Looking for

Stanley Wells is one of the Shakespeare scholars. His new book, written with characteristic verve and accessibility, considers how far sexual meaning in Shakespeare's writing is a matter of interpretation by actors, directors and critics. Tracing interpretations of Shakespearian bawdy and innuendo from eighteenth-century editors to modern scholars and critics, Wells pays special attention to recent sexually oriented studies of *A Midsummer Night's Dream*, once regarded as the most innocent of its author's plays. He considers the sonnets, some of which are addressed to a man, and asks whether they imply same-sex desire in the author, or are quasi-dramatic projections of the writer's imagination. Finally, he looks at how male-to-male relationships in the plays have been interpreted as sexual in both criticism and performance. Stanley Wells's lively, provocative and open-minded new book will appeal to a broad readership of students, theatregoers and Shakespeare lovers.

STANLEY WELLS has devoted most of his life to teaching, editing and writing about Shakespeare and his contemporaries. He was Director of the Shakespeare Institute from 1987 to 1997. He is General Editor of the Oxford editions of Shakespeare, edited *King Lear* for the multi-volume Oxford Shakespeare, and has been associated with the New Penguin edition, for which he edited several plays, since its inception. His publications include *Shakespeare: A Dramatic Life*, *Shakespeare: For All Time* (2002) and (with Paul Edmondson) *Shakespeare's Sonnets* (forthcoming in 2004). He is editor of *Shakespeare on the Stage: An Anthology of Criticism*, with E. A. Davies of *Shakespeare and the Moving Image*, with Michael Dobson of *The Oxford Companion to Shakespeare*, with Margreta de Grazia of *The Cambridge Companion to Shakespeare*, with Sarah Stanton of *The Cambridge Companion to Shakespeare on Stage*, and with Lena Orlin of *Shakespeare: An Oxford Guide*.

To my friends the actors

Looking for
Sex in Shakespeare

STANLEY WELLS

CAMBRIDGE
UNIVERSITY PRESS

PUBLISHED BY THE PRESS SYNDICATE OF THE UNIVERSITY OF CAMBRIDGE
The Pitt Building, Trumpington Street, Cambridge, United Kingdom

CAMBRIDGE UNIVERSITY PRESS
The Edinburgh Building, Cambridge, CB2 2RU, UK
40 West 20th Street, New York, NY 10011–4211, USA
477 Williamstown Road, Port Melbourne, VIC 3207, Australia
Ruiz de Alarcón 13, 28014 Madrid, Spain
Dock House, The Waterfront, Cape Town 8001, South Africa

http://www.cambridge.org

First published 2004

Printed in the United Kingdom at the University Press, Cambridge

Typeface Fournier 12/15 pt   *System* LaTeX 2ε   [TB]

A catalogue record for this book is available from the British Library

ISBN 0 521 83284 5 hardback
ISBN 0 521 54039 9 paperback

Contents

v

Illustrations

Foreword

A glaring omission from an otherwise compendious *Oxford Companion to Shakespeare* is an entry that should appear between Orson Welles and Arnold Wesker. If any scholar deserves inclusion in a reference work about Shakespeare on the page and on the stage it is Stanley Wells.

In autumn 2002, Professor Wells accepted the International Shakespeare Globe Fellowship, one of two annual fellowships that have been offered to scholars by Globe Education since 1997. As Fellow, Professor Wells gave lectures to undergraduates studying at the Globe and to MA students on the Globe/King's College MA. In addition he gave three public lectures as part of Globe Education's *Sonnets and Desire* season of staged readings, lectures and events.

In introducing his three lectures, *Lewd Interpreters*, *The Originality of Shakespeare's Sonnets* and *Men Loving Men in Shakespeare's Plays*, Lord Alexander of Weedon QC, Michael Dobson and I paid tribute to Professor Wells's work in Stratford-upon-Avon with the Royal Shakespeare Company, the Shakespeare Institute, the Shakespeare Birthplace Trust and the International Shakespeare Association, to his contribution to textual, literary and performance studies and to his support, as a trustee, of Southwark's Rose Theatre and Shakespeare's Globe.

Professor Wells has the remarkable gift of effortlessly engaging groundlings and university wits alike with his scholarship, without being patronizing or rarified. His delivery is akin to a performance and the lectures were written and presented with a live audience in mind.

Those who attended the lectures and asked afterwards for transcripts (and the many who were unable to secure a ticket) will be grateful to Sarah Stanton for promoting the idea of a publication to Cambridge University Press. However, while the three talks were written for the one-hour traffic of a lecture theatre, Professor Wells has been able to reinstate cuts made for the evening and add post-production thoughts for this published edition. Those in the original audience will miss the pleasure that the lectures afforded us when they were presented with the soul of lively action, but as readers they and others will benefit from this newly imprinted and enlarged record.

As Thomas Heywood wrote in his preface to *Greene's Tu Quoque*, 'since it hath passed the test of the stage with so general an applause, pity it were but it should likewise have the honour of the press'.

Patrick Spottiswoode
Director, Globe Education

Preface

This little book has its origins in three lectures given at Shakespeare's Globe, London, in October and November 2002. I am immensely grateful to the Globe's Director of Education, Patrick Spottiswoode, for the invitation to speak and for his genial hosting of these occasions. He kindly took the chair for the first, Professor Michael Dobson for the second, and Lord Alexander of Weedon for the third. Dr Paul Edmondson read quotations for the lecture printed as Chapter Two. I am indebted to the librarians of the Shakespeare Centre, Stratford-upon-Avon, for help with the illustrations. Dr Jan Sewell assisted in preparing the book for publication, and Sarah Stanton, of Cambridge University Press, has been unfailingly helpful at all stages of its publication.

Quotations from Shakespeare's works refer to the Oxford edition of the *Complete Works*, General Editors Stanley Wells and Gary Taylor (1986). Quotations from Shakespeare's contemporaries are modernized unless there is special reason to preserve the conventions of presentation in the original text.

Introduction

So much sex is readily apparent in Shakespeare that it might seem surprising that anyone should look for more. Virtually every play is shot through with sexual puns. The verbally fastidious fantasy of *Love's Labour's Lost* incorporates a passage (4.1.124–38) so indelicate that it might raise a blush on the cheek of many a modern playwright. In *Romeo and Juliet* the lovers' romance is counterpointed by the earthiness of the Nurse and the witty bawdy of Mercutio. In both parts of *Henry IV* and in *Pericles* scenes are set in brothels. The Vienna of *Measure for Measure* teems with lechery and vice. Yet modern critics continue to comb the plays for more, to seek out sexuality in previously unsuspected places and to attribute indecent meanings to characters who might, if they were able to react, be aghast to know of them. In the theatre, lewd meanings have been sought out, relationships once thought to be innocent have been trawled for sexual undertones, and both the comic and the serious aspects of sexual behaviour have been stressed in ways that shift the interpretative balance of the plays in which they occur.

The phenomenon extends to the poems, too. The eroticism of *Venus and Adonis* that helped to make it so popular among Shakespeare's contemporaries has been emphasized and reinterpreted in lurid ways by practitioners of gender studies and of what has come to be known as queer theory. And sexual readings of the sonnets have provoked reassessment

1

not only of the poems themselves but of Shakespeare's own sexuality.

Though it is natural to ask whether things have gone too far, it is no part of my intention in this book to deny the legitimacy of fresh explorations of Shakespeare's rich, abundant and often comic celebration of the many and varied aspects of human sexuality. Nor do I seek to question the right of the theatre to reappropriate the plays as documents that can reflect the concerns of modern society even if, while doing so, it attributes to them meanings that Shakespeare could not have envisaged. But I do want to increase self-consciousness about precisely what we are doing as both readers and performers.

My first chapter, 'Lewd interpreters', focuses on scholarly, theatrical and critical interpretations of *A Midsummer Night's Dream* in an attempt to distinguish legitimate readings-between-the-lines from over-readings that are ahistorical and sometimes untheatrical in imposing upon the texts meanings that must originate rather in the minds of the interpreters than of the dramatist. When, it asks, do sexual interpretations proceed from what would once have been considered the 'dirty minds' of the interpreters rather than from the imaginations of the dramatist and of his early audiences? Many relationships in Shakespeare's plays may be, but are not necessarily, sexual. Did Hamlet go to bed with Ophelia, as he visibly does in Kenneth Branagh's film? ('Invariably, in *my* company' is said to have been the reaction to this question of some actor-manager of the past.) Was Gertrude Claudius's lover before her husband's death? And is Bottom to be assumed to have sex with Titania?

The idea that some readings are more legitimate than others raises fundamental questions about theatrical interpretation.

The meanings of works of art are stimulated and guided by the mind of the artist but exist finally only in the minds of those who experience them. The performative arts are peculiarly susceptible to variation because, while they do not truly live until they are performed, each performance is a palimpsest created by the interaction between the written text, its lived realization, and its audience. Even in our own time, let alone with works from the past, authors have no ultimate control over the ways in which their work is realized. Directors, designers, actors and all the other personnel involved in the creation of the theatrical experience help to shape its impact, making each performance a unique event. The experience will differ according to the composition of the audience. To put it at its simplest, a production of *King Lear* given in an old people's home would make a very different impact from one given before an audience of primary school children. *Measure for Measure* would strike a Muslim audience differently from a Christian one.[1] In 1989 Mark Rylance, working with a psychiatrist, Dr Murray Cox, performed *Hamlet* to an audience of patients at Broadmoor which included serial murderers. The result was transformational for both actors and audience.[2]

Productions will affect individual members of an audience in different ways, too. Shakespeare knew this: Hamlet could rightly calculate that a representation of the murder of Gonzago would cause Claudius to react in a different way from, say, Ophelia or Horatio. In modern audiences, a twin might feel special sympathy with Viola and Sebastian in *Twelfth Night* or with the Antipholuses and Dromios in *The Comedy of Errors*. *The Merchant of Venice* has inevitably proved especially sensitive to predominantly Jewish audiences. And, to take circumstances that are relevant especially to the third of these chapters, the sexual orientation of individual spectators will affect their reactions. Lesbians might be especially interested in the relationship between Celia and Rosalind in *As You Like It* or in the characterization of Emilia in *The Two Noble Kinsmen*; the same play portrays in its title characters a pair of men to whom male homosexuals might respond with special sympathy. In a dialogue full of erotic intensity, Arcite, alone in prison with Palamon, says 'We are one another's wife, ever begetting / New births of love'; a little later Palamon asks 'Is there record of any two that loved / Better than we do, Arcite?'

> ARCITE   Sure there cannot.
> PALAMON
> I do not think it possible our friendship
> Should ever leave us.
> ARCITE   Till our deaths it cannot,
> And after death our spirits shall be led
> To those that love eternally. (2.2.80–115)

But even as they speak, Emilia, with whom they are both about to fall in love, comes upon the scene.

The personality, physique and costuming of the performers, too, will have sexual implications. Directors have been known to ensure that actors – male or female – with especially charismatic sexual appeal appear in a state of semi-, or even total, nudity at some point in their productions. It has become common to experiment with cross-dressing, testing the implications of casting males in female roles – as invariably happened in the original performances – and females in male roles. When a male actor known to be homosexual plays Richard II, his relationship with his favourites and with Aumerle is liable to take on special significance. In Ian Judge's Stratford production of *Troilus and Cressida* (1996) the leather costumes and bared buttocks of the Grecian warriors were inescapably homoerotic in their implications.

Variability of interpretation in sexual as in other respects is enhanced by the fact that plays – unlike, say, novels or poems – are peculiarly susceptible to textual alteration. Sometimes this may be for practical reasons, to do for example with availability of actors, desired length of performance, textual obscurity and even censorship. But it may also result, whether consciously or not, from a desire to promulgate specific points of interpretation. In the past censorship was commonly practised, reducing or eliminating the overt sexuality of passages such as the opening dialogue of the servants in *Romeo and Juliet*, the conversation on virginity between Helen and Paroles in *All's Well that Ends Well*, or Leontes's sexual delusions in *The Winter's Tale*. Since the sixties it has been common to emphasize sexuality or to seek it out where it had not previously been suspected. Not many directors nowadays add lines, but abbreviation is common and may slew the direction of the play in significant ways. Choice of setting, costume, and stage business can transform a scene. In Gregory Doran's production of *Timon of Athens* (Stratford, 1999) the masque, previously often used for a display of heterosexual lasciviousness, became a homosexual festival. As John Jowett writes,

> Doran's Cupidesque 'Amazons' were played by men wearing thongs and little black masks and large white feather wings. They descended from aloft to the accompaniment of [Duke] Ellington's music, firing flirtatious arrows from silly bows at Timon's guests, then taking partners in an all-male dance . . . Doran introduced a violent homoerotic mime sequence in which one of the male dancers in the masque flirted with

5

1. *A Midsummer Night's Dream*, 3.1: Titania (Stella Gonet) prepares Bottom (Desmond Barrit) for his journey to her bower in Adrian Noble's production, Royal Shakespeare Theatre, 1994

Alcibiades' soldier but rejected him when he made a pass at him at the end of Sc. 2; the disgruntled soldier later stabbed the dancer and killed him.[3]

All this was achieved with no change to the text.

Less extensive use of body language and stage business can play its part (Fig. 1). In Adrian Noble's 1994 Stratford production of *A Midsummer Night's Dream* Titania beckoned Bottom into the large upturned umbrella that represented her bower, and as it ascended we were treated to the sight of Desmond Barrit's ample posterior lunging energetically up and down in a manner that left no doubt about the relationship between the weaver and the Fairy Queen. The intonation of a single word can do its work: in Michael Boyd's Stratford production of the same play (1999), Titania's offer of a 'venturous fairy' to bring Bottom 'new nuts' unmistakably conveyed (to most members of the audience) the sense 'testicles'. And even a silence can carry innuendo. In the same play, Bottom, waking from his dream, says 'Methought I was – there is no man can tell what. Methought I was, and methought I had – but man is but a patched fool if he will offer to say what methought I had' (4.1.8–11). The innocent interpretation of 'Methought I had' is 'I thought I had ass's ears.' But, again in Noble's production, Barrit filled in the silence between 'methought I had' and 'but man is but a patched fool . . .' by peering down his pants in a manner that recalled to some members of the audience Jan Kott's remark that 'Since antiquity and up to the Renaissance the ass was credited with the strongest sexual potency and among all the quadrupeds is supposed to have the longest and hardest phallus.'[4]

Inevitably these and similar interpretative decisions raise questions of legitimacy. Is it right to convey significances that could not have been in the mind of the author as he wrote? Is it, on the other hand, impossible to deny them? How free can we be in our handling of texts from the past? Nahum Tate's drastically adapted version of *King Lear* (1681) and Colley Cibber's of *Richard III* (1700) are now usually mentioned only to be derided, but are they all that different in kind from adaptation achieved rather by production devices than by textual changes? Might it be argued that a director working for a subsidized company much patronized by schoolchildren who are studying a text for examination purposes has a duty to present that text with a minimum of mediation? Or conversely, is it more important to display the

full range of what may result from the interplay between a creative imagination of the past and an interpretative imagination
of the present? Where does interpretation end and re-creation –
or, to use a less favourable term, distortion – begin? There are
no absolute answers to these questions, but it is healthy to raise
them.

Writings meant to be read rather than performed are also, if to a
lesser degree, subject to fluctuating interpretation. Shakespeare's
sonnets, considered in the second of these chapters, are the subject
of an ongoing controversy about their sexual implications. In
them, Shakespeare defies convention by idealizing male love
objects and deploring his sexual entanglement with a female.
Are those sonnets that are addressed to and concerned with a
young man purely platonic in their orientation, reflections of a
lost Renaissance ideal of non-sexual friendship, or do they imply
same-sex desire? If so, are we to assume that the desire was
reciprocated? And, beyond this, was it consummated?

Of greater interest still in relation to Shakespeare's biography,
do the sonnets reflect his personal experience? Was he himself
'in love' with a man – or with more than one young man? Do the
sonnets imply same-sex desire in the author, or are they rather
quasi-dramatic projections of the imagination of a writer who
had a consummate ability to imagine himself into minds different
from his own? The second chapter in this book addresses these
questions in part by looking at Shakespeare's collection in relation
to other sonnet sequences of his time. It does not attempt to deny
that poems, like plays, may provoke varying reactions in the great
variety of readers. Critics of the past tended homophobically to
resist any notion that Shakespeare could have portrayed sexuality
in the relationship between the poet – or his persona – and the
young man (or men) whom he addresses. More recent readers

may have swung too far in the opposite direction in their efforts to present a liberated Shakespeare. Or, by expressing what these poems mean to them, these readers may simply show that the reading of poems, like the performing of plays, involves creative interaction between the words on the page and the sensibility that apprehends them.

The third chapter considers to what extent the plays can be interpreted as portraying sexual relationships between men. On the surface, they scarcely do so. They were written at a time when sodomy was a capital offence. Few plays of the period directly portray homosexual relationships (the most obvious and best-known example of one that does is Christopher Marlowe's *Edward II*). But such relationships existed in real life – King James I himself was notorious for his conduct with his favourites. From the beginnings of Shakespeare's career, in *The Two Gentlemen of Verona*, to the end of it, in *The Two Noble Kinsmen*, his plays are full of close, loving, even passionate male friendships. In avoiding explicit sexuality, was Shakespeare merely keeping himself out of trouble? How legitimate is it to read sex between the lines? When did the theatre and readers start to make homosexual interpretations explicit? What is the relationship between critical interpretation and theatrical projection of homosexuality in the plays? These and other questions are addressed by way of a survey of homosexual interpretations on page and stage.

CHAPTER ONE

Lewd interpreters

'Fie, what a question's that / If thou wert near a lewd interpreter!' says Portia to Nerissa in *The Merchant of Venice* after Nerissa has asked 'shall we turn to men?' (3.4.79–81). In these words Shakespeare unambiguously draws his audience's attention to a bawdy double meaning. In his time that phrase – double meaning – seems not to have been used in its modern sense – what the *Oxford English Dictionary* (*OED*) calls 'the use of an ambiguous word or phrase . . . to convey an indelicate meaning', but rather to have harked back to the ambiguous responses of the Delphic oracle, as in *All's Well that Ends Well*, where Bertram says that Paroles has deceived him 'like a double-meaning prophesier' (4.3.102–3). The nearest Shakespeare comes to using the sense for which we, if we are to make ourselves entirely clear, use the significantly French phrase 'double entendre' is in *Much Ado About Nothing*, when Benedick sets about interpreting Beatrice's words 'Against my will I am sent to bid you come in to dinner': 'Ha! "Against my will I am sent to bid you come in to dinner". There's a double meaning in that' (2.3.235–46). And the French 'double entendre' is not recorded as an anglicism before 1673. Nevertheless, indecent – or, to use a slightly less loaded term, sexually suggestive – double meanings abound in Shakespeare's plays, and in both the dramatic and the non-dramatic literature of his time.

Identification of sexual wordplay is often a complicated business. No one would doubt that Nerissa's question might be lewdly interpreted even without the pointer provided by Portia's response (in which she deplores lewdness of interpretation while simultaneously displaying it), and there are a great many other moments in Shakespeare's poems and plays at which no one could deny that Shakespeare is inviting his hearers to recognize bawdy significance in lines or dialogue that could on the face of it be taken innocently. Take, for example, a few lines in that very bawdy play *Romeo and Juliet*. Mercutio says to the Nurse, 'the bawdy hand of the dial is now upon the prick of noon' (2.3.104–5). The word 'prick' could mean simply, as *OED* puts it, one 'of the marks by which the circumference of a dial is divided', but when one considers that this is a rare meaning, that we have already been alerted to the likelihood of indecent metaphor by the word 'bawdy' used of a bodily part (the hand), and that the Nurse responds to Mercutio's words with 'Out upon you, what a man are you!', we have to acknowledge that it would be a very innocent hearer indeed who could fail to recognize in 'prick' an allusion to a quite other bodily part (Fig. 2). (Eric Partridge, incidentally, in his book *Shakespeare's Bawdy*, writes of this sentence as 'not only one of the "naughtiest" but also one of the three or four most scintillating of all Shakespeare's sexual witticisms', one whose 'full subtlety and . . . profound eroticism will, even by the witty, be grasped only by reading and pondering' certain entries in his Glossary: 'Verbal wit and witty eroticism can hardly be keener, go further, than in Mercutio's twelve-worded sentence.'[1] What, I ask myself, have I been missing?)

Very slightly less self-evident is the bawdy a little later in the same scene in an interchange between the Nurse and her servant

2. *Romeo and Juliet*: 'Out upon you, what a man are you!'; the Nurse (Edith Evans) responds to being teased by Mercutio (Ian Bannen) in Glen Byam Shaw's production, the Royal Shakespeare Theatre, 1961

Peter: 'And thou must stand by, too,' she says, 'and suffer every knave to use me at his pleasure' (2.3.145–6). This could – just – mean nothing more than 'You too have to hang around letting any rogue treat me as he pleases'; perhaps the performer of the Nurse should act as if she – or he – were unconscious of the possibility of a bawdy interpretation of her – or his – words, but we ourselves can scarcely remain oblivious to this possibility when Peter responds with 'I saw no man use you at his pleasure. If I had, my weapon should quickly have been out . . .', with its obvious play on the word 'weapon'. Still, it is just conceivable that an unsophisticated hearer might fail to pick up the innuendo.

Those are two pretty certain instances of primarily hetero-sexual bawdy in *Romeo and Juliet* (though with a boy playing the Nurse it might not have been exclusively heterosexual), and we can be in no doubt that Shakespeare consciously intended his hearers to recognize it. There are many other points in the plays to which sexual significance has been attributed by modern critics but where wordplay is not activated by devices such as the Nurse's outraged reaction to Mercutio's wordplay on 'prick' or by Peter's repetition of her words 'use [me] at his pleasure.' At a climactic moment of *Antony and Cleopatra*, for example, Cleopatra says 'Husband, I come' (5.2.282). Antony is dead; Cleopatra is preparing to join him 'Where souls do couch on flowers' (4.15.41). It is the first time she has referred to him as 'husband'. The words can be taken in a purely literal sense. In re-cent times, however, it has often been suggested that 'come' plays on the sense 'experience orgasm', even though there is nothing in the text to activate a pun. The matter has been debated. Adrian Colman, in his book *The Dramatic Use of Bawdy in Shakespeare* (1974), denies wordplay because he finds no other use of this particular sense in Shakespeare. He does, however, bring forward a perfectly clear instance of it in one of Shakespeare's contemporaries – 'a maid that will come with a wet finger', in Dekker's *The Honest Whore*, Part One (1.2.4)[2] – while claiming that this 'does not make it Shakespearean'. Gordon Williams, in his *Glossary of Shakespeare's Sexual Language*, admits the sense but supports it only with a reference to *Much Ado About Nothing* where Benedick, responding to Margaret's statement that Beatrice 'hath legs', responds 'And therefore will come' (5.2.23–4). If the meaning was available to members of Shakespeare's audience they might, however subliminally, have been conscious of it as an innuendo as Cleopatra spoke her words, whether or not it was in Shakespeare's mind as he wrote. And it would be possible – though, in my view, highly distasteful – for the performer to speak the word in a manner suggestive of innuendo.

There are other points where the speaker's unconsciousness of bawdy undertones that may nevertheless be picked up by the audience is part of the joke – Dogberry declares himself to be 'as pretty a piece of flesh as any is in Messina' (*Much Ado About Nothing*, 4.2.79–80). And there are also countless other points at which it would be unreasonable to doubt that bawdy – whether comic or not – is intended even though there are no explicit textual pointers to it.

Bawdy language is often associated in the plays with 'low' comic characters, such as the rarely materialized Clown in *Othello*, with his gross wordplay on 'wind instruments' and 'tail', which reflects back to arouse associations of venereal disease – 'the Neapolitan bone-ache' – on his suggestion that the musicians' instruments have 'been in Naples'.

> CLOWN Why, masters, ha' your instruments been in
> Naples, that they speak i'th' nose thus?
> MUSICIAN How, sir, how?

CLOWN   Are these, I pray you, wind instruments?
MUSICIAN   Ay, marry are they, sir.
CLOWN   O, thereby hangs a tail.
MUSICIAN   Whereby hangs a tale?
CLOWN   Marry, sir, by many a wind instrument that I
   know. (3.1.3–11)

Or take Cloten's statement, in a not dissimilar episode in *Cymbeline*, that music is said to 'penetrate'. On its own the word here might mean no more than 'pierce the ear, heart, or feelings of' (*OED* 3a), as it innocently does in *The Two Gentlemen of Verona*:

Sad sighs, deep groans, nor silver-shedding tears
Could penetrate her uncompassionate sire. (3.1.228–9)

But coming from Cloten, who is already established as a gross-minded buffoon, and followed by the words 'If you can penetrate her with your fingering, so; we'll try with tongue too' (2.3.13–14), the sexual implications must be apparent to all but the most innocent hearers. And, as numerous critics, from, at least, M. M. Mahood in her classic *Shakespeare's Wordplay* (1957) onwards, have repeatedly demonstrated, sexual wordplay need not be comic and may emerge, if not from the mouths of babes and sucklings, at least from those of romantic heroines such as Viola, Desdemona and the fourteen-year-old Juliet; and, even when it is comic, it may be delicately, slyly and touchingly so rather than coarsely and obscenely. The matter of tone, always difficult to define, is crucial to interpretation, in the theatre no less than in the study.

A mass of effort has been devoted to the attempt to identify Shakespearian bawdy – and even sometimes to add to it. Restoration adaptations sometimes exaggerated bawdy aspects of the plays, rather perhaps by innuendo than by Shakespeare's more intellectually charged wordplay, as in Dryden's version of *The Tempest* when Miranda brings a sword and salve to the wounded Hippolito. 'I am come to ease you', she says, unwrapping the sword; he replies 'Alas! I feel the cold air come to me. / My wound shoots worse than ever.' Miranda 'wipes and anoints the sword', asking 'Does it still grieve you?' Hippolito responds 'Now methinks there's something laid just upon it.'

MIRANDA Do you find no ease?
HIPPOLITO Yes, yes, upon the sudden all the pain
Is leaving me. Sweet heaven, how am I eased! (5.2.59–65)[3]

Far more explicitly crude is Thomas Duffett's *The Mock-Tempest or The Enchanted Castle*, of 1674, which burlesques the production of Shadwell's adaptation in a particularly scurrilous manner. Set in a brothel instead of a desert island, it is throughout, as Gerard Langbaine observed as early as 1691, 'intermixed with so much scurrility' as to 'offend the modest mind'.[4] Here, for instance, is Prospero giving Miranda her first sight of a young man:

PROSPERO Advance the frizzled frouzes of thine eyes, and
   gloat on yon fair thing.
MIRANDA O dear sweet father, is that a ho- ho- ho- a
   horse-man – husband?
PROSPERO It is, my girl, and a yerker too. I'faith, were he
   not tired with seeking of his company, he would play
   thee such horse-tricks would make thee sneer again.
MIRANDA 'Tis the most 'crumptious thing; I'vads, if
   you'll let me have it, I'll make no more dirt pies, nor eat
   the chalk you score with.[5]

The modest mind of F. J. Furnivall was so much offended by this passage that, quoting it in a collection of Shakespeare allusions, he added, in square brackets, 'and so on, the vulgar beast'. 'As pearls before swine', wrote Furnivall, 'so were Shakespeare's plays in the eyes of the hog Duffett.'[6]

Over the centuries, scholars, especially editors concerned with the minutiae of the text, have identified bawdy, sometimes deploring it, occasionally even removing it. Pope and some later editors of *Romeo and Juliet* omitted Mercutio's lines now printed in up-to-date editions as

> O Romeo, that she were, O that she were
> An open-arse, and thou a popp'rin' pear. (2.1.37–8)

'Open-arse', it has to be admitted, is a twentieth-century editorial extrapolation from the 'open, or' of Q2 and 'open *Et* Caetera' of Q1, but the import of the passage is clear enough without it. Charles Knight expressed contempt that the lines should have been omitted by Pope, 'Who', he says, 'in *The Rape of the Lock*, has introduced one couplet, at least, that would have disgraced the age of Elizabeth' – I suppose he's thinking of the lines: 'Men prove with child as powerful fancy works, / And maids turned bottles call aloud for corks' (Canto 4, ll. 53–4); nevertheless, Knight too omitted the lines from Mercutio's speech with the weird excuse that 'they can only interest the verbal critic'. At the same time, however, Knight sought to exculpate his timorous inconsistency by boasting 'we distinctly record their omission'.[7] This provoked the German critic Delius to remark, snidely but justly, that the lines have 'hurt the delicacy of some of the English critics to such an extent, that the latter have omitted them from the text, which without them is unintelligible, in order thereby to give them the greater prominence in their notes'.[8]

Eighteenth-century editors such as George Steevens and Edmond Malone identified the bawdy undertones in many passages where they may not be immediately apparent but are now

17

accepted as authentic, such as Hamlet's '*coun*try matters' and his punning on 'show': 'Will a tell us what this show meant' says Ophelia, to which Hamlet replies 'Ay, or any show that you'll show him' (3.2.136–7). They even sometimes ascribed sexual significances that are denied by modern scholars; so for example Thomas Hanmer supposed that, in Lear's 'The goodyear shall devour them, flesh and fell' (5.3.24), 'goodyear' was a form of an alleged French word, *goujeres*, which Hanmer appears to have invented.[9] He ascribed to it the meaning 'venereal disease', arguing for it with what Gordon Williams calls 'all the ingenuity and surface plausibility so often met with in present-day kite-flying'.[10]

Scholars of the eighteenth century and later were not always tolerant of what they found; Johnson considered that 'he who does not understand' Mercutio's quibbles 'needs not lament his ignorance',[11] and it was not uncommon to protect Shakespeare's reputation with the suggestion that offensive passages, such as the Porter's speech in *Macbeth*, had been interpolated by actors. This attitude finds classic expression in Robert Bridges's essay 'On the Influence of the Audience', which first appeared in the last volume of the splendid Shakespeare Head edition of A. H. Bullen of 1904–7; though his essay is not primarily concerned with language, Bridges maintains an essentially similar point of view to that of earlier expurgators such as Thomas Bowdler and Charles Lamb: 'Shakespeare should not be put into the hands of the young without the warning that the foolish things in his plays were written to please the foolish, the filthy for the filthy, and the brutal for the brutal . . .'[12]

Even in the eighteenth century, theatre texts of the plays had often been expurgated to some degree. There was an odd belief that words might be fit to be read in silence but not to be spoken in public. Bell's theatre edition of 1773–5 reprints the prompt books of the Theatres Royal at Drury Lane and Covent Garden for plays in the repertory, but the editor adds additional suggestions for cuts, in order to avoid 'offence to decency' in, for instance, Iago's obscenities in the opening scene of *Othello*. I suppose, however, that the first attempt at a systematic identification of the bawdy in Shakespeare's plays was made, oddly enough, by the chaste-minded Henrietta, sister of Thomas Bowdler, as a preliminary to preparing the first twenty plays in the notorious 'Family Shakspeare, in which nothing is added to the original text, but those words and expressions are omitted which cannot with propriety be read aloud in a family'. Perhaps unfortunately, the result of her study can only be negatively inferred from the excisions made in the edition, which first appeared in four volumes in 1807; publication was anonymous, perhaps, as Gary Taylor suggests, as a way of protecting her reputation by not admitting to have 'understood things that no decent woman should understand'.[13] Henrietta's twin brother, Thomas, completed the emasculation and accepted responsibility for it in the ten-volume edition of 1818; both editions, we may note, were published well before the Victorian era. Victorianism is a common pre-Victorian phenomenon, perhaps as a reaction against the excesses of the Regency.

Bowdler's Preface to the complete edition declares that 'Many words and expressions occur which are of so indecent a nature as to render it highly desirable that they should be erased . . . neither the vicious taste of the age, nor the most brilliant effusions of wit, can afford an excuse for profaneness or obscenity . . . To banish everything of this nature from [Shakespeare's] writings is the object of the present undertaking.'[14] There are close parallels between the Bowdlers' enterprise and that of another brother and sisterly collaboration, which also first appeared in 1807, and which also offered an adaptation of twenty of Shakespeare's plays. This is Charles and Mary Lamb's *Tales from Shakespeare*, ascribed on its first publication to Charles, whose sister's name was not added to the title page until the seventh edition, of 1838, though Charles had made clear in letters to friends that Mary wrote fourteen of the tales and that he contributed only six – the tragedies, along with 'occasionally a tail piece or correction of grammar – and *all* of the spelling'.[15] Both enterprises were undertaken in a spirit of protectiveness for the young. The Lambs, explaining that the *Tales* are written mainly for 'young ladies . . . because boys are generally permitted the use of their fathers' libraries at a much earlier age than girls are', encourage brothers to explain the hard bits to their sisters, and even to read pleasing passages from the original plays to them, 'carefully selecting what is proper for a young sister's ear'.[16] Similarly, Bowdler declares that his aim has been 'to exclude . . . whatever is unfit to be read aloud by a gentleman to a company of ladies'. He can, he says, 'hardly imagine a more pleasing occupation for a winter's evening in the country, than for a father to read one of Shakespeare's plays to his family circle. My object is to enable him to do so without incurring the danger of falling unawares among words and expressions which are of such a nature as to raise a blush on the cheek of modesty, or render it necessary for the reader to pause, and examine the sequel, before he proceeds further in the entertainment of the evening.'[17] The Lambs idealize the plots and clean up the language; there are no bawds or brothels in their *Measure for Measure* or *Pericles*, and bawdy language is almost totally expunged. They were not completely successful in their enterprise; in *The Merchant of Venice*, both Mary Lamb and Miss Bowdler retain Graziano's closing couplet about 'keeping safe Nerissa's ring'; interestingly, however, when brother Thomas came along he noticed it in time to remove it from the collected edition. He did not, however, expunge Cloten's 'penetration' passage from *Cymbeline*, presumably because he did not understand it.

Some plays posed special challenges. Although in *Othello* Bowdler changes 'your daughter and the Moor are now making the beast with two backs' (1.1.117–18) to '. . . are now together', he allows the word 'whore' to remain, prefacing the play with a warning that in it he has 'depart[ed] in some degree from the principle on which this publication is undertaken'. And *Measure for Measure* defeated him altogether: 'Feeling my own inability to render this play sufficiently correct for family-reading, I have thought it advisable to print it . . . from the published copy, as performed at the Theatre Royal, Covent Garden' – that is, from John Philip Kemble's acting version.

The Family Shakspeare was frequently reprinted, and its underlying principles undoubtedly influenced many editions intended for young people until well into the twentieth century. At least until the liberations of the 1960s, school editions were systematically bowdlerized. I remember having to teach from an edition of *Henry IV*, Part One in which so harmless a word as 'guts' was altered to 'inwards'. And even scholarly editions often ignored bawdy, or skirted nervously round it. To take a few examples at random, in *Much Ado About Nothing*, G. L. Kittredge (1941) does not annotate Margaret's 'A maid and stuffed! – there's goodly catching of cold' (3.4.60–1) or, in a later scene, her 'Give us the swords; we have bucklers of our own' (5.2.17–18). J. M. Nosworthy, in the still-current Arden *Cymbeline*, first published in 1955, ignores the word 'penetrate' and says of 'fingering' merely that 'There is a coarse pun'; even in more recent times I was surprised to have to explain to a writer on *Love's Labour's Lost* just why, in one of the lewdest passages in Shakespeare, Maria accuses Costard and others of talking 'greasily' (4.1.136); and I once heard a distinguished and broad-minded lady Shakespearian exclaim with disbelief that some people find allusions to masturbation in the sonnets – I suppose she was thinking of 'having traffic with thyself alone' in Sonnet 4, where to me (and to Helen Vendler, who writes of 'the boy's auto-erotic *traffic with [himself] alone*'[18]) it seems clear enough.

The scattered identifications of bawdy by editors and other Shakespeare specialists were supplemented during the nineteenth century and later by more general studies of language such as Henley and Farmer's seven-volume *Dictionary of Slang and its Analogues* (1890–3) and by the *Oxford English Dictionary* which, however, ignores many sexual words and expressions, as does Alexander Schmidt in his *Lexicon* (1874–5) and C. T. Onions in his *Shakespeare Glossary*, originally published in 1911 (naturally, since this is an offshoot of the *OED*). Recent editors can take advantage of the sane, scholarly but frank work of Gordon Williams in his three-volume *Dictionary of Sexual Language and Imagery in Shakespeare and Stuart Literature* (1994) and its handy offshoot, *A Glossary of Shakespeare's Sexual Language* (1997).

The search for sexual subtext in character and action as well as in language was greatly boosted in the early years of the twentieth century by the work of Sigmund Freud. In fact, Freud's discoveries had been anticipated less in intellectualized literary study than in the work of creative artists in their responses to the plays; one thinks, for instance, of the powerful eroticism in paintings based on *A Midsummer Night's Dream* by nineteenth-century artists such as Fuseli, Richard Dadd or Sir Joseph

3. 'How now, spirit, whither wander you?' *A Midsummer Night's Dream*, 2.1.1: Puck (Aidan McArdle) with Peaseblossom (Sirine Saba) in Michael Boyd's production, Royal Shakespeare Theatre, 1999

Noël Paton. Consider the photograph of a moment from the production of *A Midsummer Night's Dream* by Michael Boyd given at Stratford-upon-Avon in 1999 (Fig. 3). Needless to say, you would have seen nothing like that in nineteenth-century productions of the play. Yet it is not all that far away from the painting by Sir Joseph Nöel Paton, done during the 1840s (Fig. 4).

As the implications of Freud's work came to be absorbed into the mainstream of thought, psychoanalytical interpretations of Shakespearian characters based on explorations of the plays' sexual subtext, including the linguistic dimension, proliferated

4. *A Midsummer Night's Dream*, Puck with the First Fairy: an oil
painting by Sir Joseph Nöel Paton (1821–1901) which in its eroticism
anticipates late twentieth-century productions

both in criticism and in theatrical practice. Ernest Jones's studies
of *Hamlet*, published between 1910 and 1949, influenced both
literary and theatrical interpretation with their diagnosis that
Hamlet suffers from an Oedipus complex; the closet scene (3.4)
seems first to have featured a bed, and a nightgowned Gertrude,
in a Prague production of 1927 (Fig. 5).[19] So far as I know,
no critic or actor explicitly diagnosed homosexuality in any of
Shakespeare's characters until after Freud's work had appeared.
I shall say more about this topic in my final chapter.

Understandably, psychoanalytical interpretations of the plays,
in conjunction particularly with the close reading associated

5. *Hamlet*: the 'closet scene' (3.4), showing the bed which since 1927 has frequently figured in performances; Mark Rylance as Hamlet, Claire Higgins as Gertrude; Royal Shakespeare Theatre, 1989, directed by Ron Daniels

with critics of the 1930s such as I. A. Richards and William Empson, intensified interest in the sexual nuances of the language. This gave rise to the first attempt at a systematic, alphabetically arranged study, Eric Partridge's *Shakespeare's Bawdy*, first published in 1947, which was described by his more scholarly successor, Gordon Williams, as 'not so much a pioneer as a watershed' in that Partridge 'was the first to provide a listing simply of bawdy uses and to do so in comparatively forthright terms'.[20] The climate of the times when Partridge's book first appeared may be judged by the fact that it did so in an edition limited to 1,000 copies selling at the high price of two guineas (at a time when this sum would have bought 42 Penguins (books,

25

not biscuits)). The circumstances of its publication and certain features of the work itself aligned it with the category of erotic literature (or, in the vulgate, dirty books) such as might be perused with impunity by the wealthy and learned but should be priced out of the financial reach, and composed in a style that was out of the educational reach, of anyone else.

Partridge follows the time-honoured custom of resorting to the sanitizing influence of Latin for certain expressions which English might have rendered accessibly offensive; so we read that, in *Henry V*, in the Constable's statement that his mistress 'was not bridled' (3.7.50), 'There may even be a pun on "to put the bridal-bit in her mouth"': "*penem in vaginam inmittere*"; and, in the 'greasy' passage in *Love's Labour's Lost*, that the words 'in' and 'out' may be used 'in reference to the target or mark, the innuendo being *digitae in vulvam inmissae* (or *impositae* – or, at best, *vir sub indusio mulieris praetantans*, or not doing so'). (If you wonder what is under discussion, it's fingers being pushed into the vulva, or the man pushing under the woman's clothes.) On occasion Partridge seems even to have coined Latinisms to avoid straightforward mention of sexual activity; one of Mistress Quickly's speeches, he says, 'would seem to glance at penilingism' – a word which, apparently meaning 'tonguing the penis', is not recorded even in the most recent editions of the *OED* (though I have found it on the internet).

There is at least one sexual practice which Partridge could not bring himself to name to his readers. He deduces that Shakespeare himself was not merely exclusively heterosexual but that he

> was an exceedingly knowledgeable amorist, a versatile connoisseur, and a highly artistic, and ingeniously skilful, practitioner of love-making, who could have taught Ovid rather more than that facile doctrinaire could have taught him;

he evidently knew of, and probably he practised, an artifice accessible to few – one that I cannot becomingly mention here, though I felt it obligatory to touch on it, very briefly, in the Glossary.[21]

Scouring the Glossary to save my readers the trouble of doing so I have come to the conclusion that he means heterosexual anal intercourse, though 'artifice' seems a funny word for it.

In spite of this sort of coyness, Partridge's book helped to lead the way towards a new freedom and honesty in acknowledging and investigating the full extent of Shakespeare's linguistic range and in responding to the sexual resonances of a substantial section of his vocabulary. The floodgates opened with the liberations of the sixties. Adrian Colman's book *The Dramatic Use of Bawdy in Shakespeare*, of 1974, is the first attempt at a critical study, moderate and reasonable in tone, and including a glossary in which – as in the body of the book – Colman at times takes issue with what he calls 'inadequately supported attributions of indecencies to Shakespeare' in both Partridge and other scholars;[22] Colman is especially interesting (though, like everyone else, far from definitive) on the difficult matter of tone.

What swept through the sewer gates ten years later, in Frankie Rubinstein's *Dictionary of Shakespeare's Sexual Puns and their Significance*, is a far murkier kettle of fish. Claiming to identify 'hundreds and hundreds of still unnoted puns',[23] Rubinstein lays herself wide open to the accusation of reading with, as Colman moderately puts it in another context, 'the distorting eye of early adolescence'.[24] Time and again, in reading her entries, one has to ask oneself who is making the pun: the author (through the character), or the interpreter. Let me offer just a few illustrations, endeavouring to refrain from ironical commentary as I do so.

In *Coriolanus* (a name in itself fraught with possibilities of misunderstanding, as witnessed both by the tendency on the part of the mealy-mouthed to pronounce it as 'Coriolarnus' and by the nature of its occurrence in Cole Porter's song 'Brush up your Shakespeare': 'If she says your behaviour is heinous, / Kick her right in the Coriolanus'), the triumphant Coriolanus begs a favour of Cominius:

> I sometime lay here in Corioles
> At a poor man's house. He used me kindly.
>   . . . I request you
> To give my poor host freedom. (1.10.81–6)

In reply, Cominius declares 'Were he the butcher of my son he should / Be free as is the wind.' (The passage is, incidentally but not entirely irrelevantly, adapted from Plutarch, where Martius says 'Among the Volsces there is an old friend and host of mine, . . . who . . . liveth now a poor prisoner in the hands of his enemies; . . . it would do me great pleasure if I could save him from this one danger, to keep him from being sold as a slave.'[25]) There is nothing in Shakespeare to suggest any sexual subtext to the lines. Rubinstein (p. 31), however, glossing 'poor' in the phrase 'poor man' as wordplay on the Latin 'puer, an unmarried man, boy', declares, citing Colman and Partridge for support, that 'lay' means 'for the sex act', that 'used me kindly' means that Martius was 'used coitally', or 'sexually', by the 'poor man', now glossing 'poor' as 'pederast'. Then, picking upon Cominius's rank as General, she glosses this word as 'whore-like' with a reference to *OED* which I find difficult to fathom, stating that Cominius 'whore-like' answers with a pun, in the word 'butcher', on 'bugger'. 'If', she says, ' "butcher" means only "slaughterer" and is not a pun on "bugger", the General's charity is hardly paternal and completely bewildering.' I take it that what she really means here is 'buggerer' not 'bugger', but in any case I can see nothing odd about Cominius saying that even if Martius's host had butchered his, Cominius's, son, his gratitude to Martius is so great that he would feel obliged to yield to his request.

Skating lightly over many acres of thin ice, I alight momentarily on Rubinstein's comment on Othello's 'Come, Desdemona, I have but an hour / Of love, of worldly matter and direction / To spend with thee' (1.3.298–300). Here, Rubinstein says, 'direction' conceals (barely) a pun on 'erection'; similarly, Hamlet's 'I knew him, *Hor*atio' (5.1.180; 'Hor' italicized by Rubinstein) 'introduces the possibility that he knew this "whoreson" [Yorick] in the biblical sense, carnally.'

Rubinstein's entry on 'keen' introduces a new kind of pun (not uncommonly diagnosed in more recent critical studies), one that plays not on the English word in question, but on a translation of it into a different language, as if we are expected, as we listen, both to take in what the actor is saying and simultaneously to translate it into, say, French or Latin, or any other language which would produce the possibility of obscene wordplay.

In her entry on 'keen' Rubinstein finds this kind of thing within a short passage in *A Midsummer Night's Dream*:

LYSANDER
. . .
Transparent Helena, nature shows art
That through thy bosom makes me see thy heart.
Where is Demetrius? O, how fit a word
Is that vile name to perish on my sword!
HELENA
Do not say so, Lysander; say not so.
What though he love your Hermia? Lord, what though?
Yet Hermia still loves you; then be content.

LYSANDER

Content with Hermia? No, I do repent
The tedious minutes I with her have spent.
Not Hermia but Helena I love.
Who will not change a raven for a dove?
The will of man is by his reason swayed,
And reason says you are the worthier maid.
Things growing are not ripe until their season,
So I, being young, till now not ripe to reason.
And, touching now the point of human skill,
Reason becomes the marshal to my will,
And leads me to your eyes, where I o'erlook
Love's stories written in love's richest book.

HELENA

Wherefore was I to this keen mockery born?
When at your hands did I deserve this scorn?
Is't not enough, is't not enough, young man,
That I did never – no, nor never can –
Deserve a sweet look from Demetrius' eye,
But you must flout my insufficiency? (2.2.110–34)

Helena is, we learn, 'revolted [understandably] at Lysander's saying that the "art" (Latin *ars* / arse) of nature' (glossed as 'the genitals') 'enabled him to see the beauty of her heart' (glossed 'eart', without the h, or arse). 'Be content' (you may imagine what she does with that) she says, 'with Hermia.' From the alleged Latin pun on 'art' we move to French ones on enough (p. 88) – 'assez', signifying 'asses' – and on the adjective 'true', (p. 140) again producing 'arse' via 'trou', meaning 'hole'. In this same entry on 'keen' Rubinstein assures us that 'Shakespeare's keen mockery of sexual excitement includes many other puns on Latin *acies*, meaning keenness or sharp edge.'

A Midsummer Night's Dream, out of which Rubinstein makes such capital, was often regarded in the past as the most innocent of its author's plays, the one least likely, in Miss Bowdler's words, to 'raise a blush on the cheek of modesty', and therefore the most appropriate as a young person's introduction to the works of Shakespeare. There was a time when I thought it contained only one piece of bawdy, in the joke about 'French crowns' (1.2.88–90). That was long ago. But I still think that it is nothing like as nocent as many modern interpreters, some of them, I suspect, influenced by Rubinstein's book, allege. I want to offer extended consideration of two critical writings about this play in support of my contention that lewdness of interpretation in certain recent discussions of Shakespeare derives not from the text or from meanings that it might have held for Shakespeare's contemporaries but purely from the minds of the interpreters, and so must be regarded rather as a gratuitous imposition on the text than as an authentic interpretation of it.

What, I wonder, would Miss Bowdler have thought had she known that in 1994 there would appear a long, learned, well-written article with the title 'Bestial Buggery in *A Midsummer Night's Dream*'?[26] The author, Bruce Thomas Boehrer, acknowledges assistance from eight other scholars and tells us that much of his research was completed during a Folger Library/NEH Institute on, interestingly, 'Shakespeare and the History of Taste'. His work is supported by an appendix, 'Bestiality and the Law in Renaissance England', which provides statistical tables on 'Indictments for bestial buggery in the reigns of Elizabeth 1 and James 1' and 'Animals abused in English Renaissance bestiality indictments' (which regrettably include no asses.)

'Although no one', Boehrer writes, 'has paid much sustained attention to the fact, *A Midsummer Night's Dream* is patently about bestiality.'[27] It is a striking opening. One can almost see the headlines in the tabloids had reporters got hold of it: ' "Children's

favourite really about sex with animals" says noted scholar.'
And at a later point in the article Boehrer argues that 'bestiality
arguably encompasses a large part of the play's overt eroticism'.[28]
Once this premise has been stated, sinister significance, which
my younger self overlooked, accrues to various phrases such as
'*Use* me but as your spaniel' (2.1.205) and 'The man shall *have*
his mare again' (3.3.47–8).

No doubt the emphasis on sexuality here and elsewhere has
occurred as a reaction against sentimentalizing interpretations,
but it is perhaps not unreasonable to suggest that the winsome
phrase 'bestial buggery' affords, to say the least, an imprecise
response to the play's tonal register. The argument depends
on the belief that, as Boehrer puts it, 'the fairy king solves his
marital problems by openly transforming his wife into the erotic
bondslave of an ass', but it is at least open to argument that
the play does not imply sexual intercourse between Bottom and
Titania. There is truth in Boehrer's claim that 'the spectacle of
Titania and Bottom embracing and sleeping together comes as
close to enacted sexual intercourse as any scene in Shakespearean
comedy',[29] but intercourse is at most only to be inferred. There
was no suggestion of it in the Globe's 2002 production. We
should perhaps remember that Bottom is not really an ass, and
that although Boehrer says that 'It is Titania ... whose *humanity*
is more fundamentally impeached [than Bottom's] by the entire
exchange',[30] she is not in fact portrayed as a member of the human
race but as a fairy. She has, moreover, declared her intention
to turn Bottom into the likeness of 'an airy spirit' by purging
his 'mortal grossness' – words that Boehrer does not quote.
And, whatever Titania's fancies may be, Bottom gives no signs
of actively sharing them. He may acquiesce in her embraces,
but even Jan Kott (in a book published in 1987 in which he

repudiates some of the argument of his better-known chapter on the play in *Shakespeare Our Contemporary*), has dissociated himself from Peter Brook's emphasis in his 1970 production on sexuality, remarking that 'in the spectacle staged by Peter Brook and many of his followers which emphasizes Titania's sexual fascination with a monstrous phallus (mea culpa!) the carnival ritual of Bottom's adventure is altogether lost'. Bottom, says Kott, 'appreciates being treated as a very important person, but is more interested in the frugal pleasure of eating than in the bodily charms of Titania'.[31] And James L. Calderwood has written 'Surely a good part of Oberon's punishment of Titania centres in the physical and metaphysical impossibility of a fairy Queen to couple with an ass.'[32] If Bottom and Titania do make love, they do so as fairies, or – to quote another of Titania's epithets for Bottom – as angels do. However that may be.

Boehrer is concerned mainly with the play's overall design. 'The play's overall effect', he writes, 'is a bit like a Protestant marriage-manual constructed out of animal pornography.'[33] (Try using that as an inducement next time you invite a young friend to see the play.) If we turn (as Nerissa would have said) to discussion of *A Midsummer Night's Dream* in Patricia Parker's *Shakespeare from the Margins*, we find a critic more closely concerned with verbal detail. This is an immensely learned book, the product of a massive amount of reading and research; but I cannot help feeling that its author overplays lewdness of interpretation. All the 'rude mechanicals', she says, are 'furnished with names that suggest their erotic counterparts'. Snug the joiner 'insists (in the passage that plays on gnomon [i.e. a carpenter's square], *nomen*, and no man) that he is "a man as other men are . . ."', evoking 'the "fit" or snug joinery that . . . links sexual fitting or joining with carpentry'.[34] That sounds very convincing until we ask what is this passage in which the simple Snug is said to play so learnedly on words?[35] Actually it's not spoken by Snug at all, but by Bottom putting words into Snug's mouth:

> . . . half his face must be seen through the lion's neck, and he himself must speak through, saying thus or to the same defect: 'ladies', or 'fair ladies, I would wish you' or 'I would request you' or 'I would entreat you not to fear, not to tremble. My life for yours. If you think I come hither as a lion, it were pity of my life. No, I am no such thing. I am a man, as other men are' – and there, indeed, let him name his name, and tell them plainly he is Snug the joiner. (3.1.33–42)

And where is the wordplay that Parker finds on 'gnomon, *nomen*, and no man'? There is none. The words 'no man' do not appear in conjunction in this passage – or anywhere else in the play spoken by Snug.

What about the other mechanicals? We may doubt that 'weaver' actually is 'homophonically "wiver"' while allowing that 'Bottom the weaver . . . recalls in his name the phallic shape of the *bottom*, or core, on which a weaver's yarn was wound' (p. 95). At the same time we may object that nothing is done to draw our attention to the resemblance, any more than to the fact that Francis Flute's surname was 'slang for the male member'. Surely a more relevant association for the name Flute in connection with an adolescent who has 'a beard coming' is the high-pitched musical instrument. There are times when a flute is a flute just as a pipe is a pipe – unless you are a determinedly lewd interpreter. And to my mind it is over-fanciful to find 'suggestions of the sexually liberal or promiscuous in *Francis* or *frank*'. There is nothing in the dialogue to suggest that the timorous Francis is lewdly inclined, nor is any joke made about his name.

Must every Francis – such as Friar Francis in *Much Ado About Nothing* – be suspected of promiscuity merely by virtue of his name?

Then we are told that 'Snout the tinker (the artisan who plays both Wall and "Wall's hole" . . .) evokes bawdy jests about the tinker who serves maids to "stop up their holes".'[36] The phrase 'stop up their holes' is given in quotation marks; an unwary reader might suppose it to be a quotation from the play. It is not. In fact it is an extract from an old, anonymous ballad.[37] We are on even less firm ground with Peter Quince, surrounded, we are told, by 'a similar phallic suggestiveness'. The critic prints his forename in inverted commas as if to nudge us into perceiving a double entendre. Peter is, I am told, used in the United States as a slang word for the penis, but this sense, according to Eric Partridge in his *Dictionary of Historical Slang*,[38] was current in England only from the middle of the nineteenth century and is now obsolete. Williams does not list it. And Quince's last name, we are told, 'recalls the wedge-shaped *quines* or quoins used for building houses'. I puzzled over this sentence before realizing that the key-word must be 'wedge-shaped'. Wedge-shaped. Well, it takes all sorts to make a world. And I confess I am still puzzling over Starveling, whose 'thinness . . . explains why, within this predominantly phallic mode of naming, he takes only female parts'.

Finally, we are asked to believe that 'As Thomas Clayton and others have pointed out' (on the well-known scholarly principle that if someone else has said something, however silly, it must be true) '. . . the double- (or multiple-) meaning sexual references associated both with these players and with the chink and hole of their play-within-a-play also unambiguously evade the homo/hetero divide, suggesting (ungrammatically) neither an

exclusively heterosexual reference nor any single bodily orifice.'
'It is therefore appropriate', the critic continues, 'that when Peter
Quince assigns the roles for the "show" [in presumably meaning-
ful inverted commas – are we expected to understand a menstrual
show?] they are to perform before their superiors, he instructs
the artisan-players as follows – "masters, here are your parts,
and I am to entreat you, request you, and desire you, to con them
by tomorrow night" . . . lines whose ambiguous "parts," in prox-
imity to "con," suggest the conning of parts both dramatic *and*
sexual, a link repeated in the description of this show as "conn'd
with cruel pain" . . . and the sexual (and class) overtones of "to
do you service".'[39] Surely what Parker is doing here is dredging
a sentence for all conceivable alternative bawdy meanings, drag-
ging them to the surface, and yoking them together in a pattern
that is of the critic's, not the dramatist's, making. I shudder to
think what winkings, nudgings, leering and lewd gestures would
be resorted to by actors who took notice of this kind of criticism.

When I was a schoolteacher it was often observed that the
naughty boys and girls would sit at the back of the classroom
sniggering and giggling amongst themselves whenever the
teacher said anything that might be remotely open to lewdness of interpretation. Now, it seems, the lewd interpreters have
moved up in the world and are regaling their students and
fellow-scholars in exactly the same way. The kind of criticism
of which I have been speaking is currently fashionable. Many
more examples could be given, from both sides of the Atlantic.
It is pursued with the appearance, at least, of scholarly rigour
and critical sophistication. But I suggest that it is in the same line
of descent as other kinds of criticism, now far from fashionable,
with which the critics I have cited, and others like them, might
well not wish to be associated. Some forty years ago, Jan Kott,

describing *A Midsummer Night's Dream* as 'the most erotic of Shakespeare's plays', imagined Titania's court 'consisting of old men and women, toothless and shaking, their mouths wet with saliva, who sniggeringly procure a monster for their mistress'. He visualized Titania as 'a very tall, flat and fair girl, with long arms and legs, resembling the white Scandinavian girls I used to see in rue de la Harpe, or rue Huchette, walking and clinging tightly to negroes with faces grey or so black that they were almost undistinguishable from the night'. And, virtually admitting the inappropriateness of his reading to the play, he expressed surprise that 'the scenes between Titania and Bottom transformed into an ass are often played for laughs in the theatre'.[40] Kott's failure of theatrical imagination is the product of fantasy – of his use of the text to release extraordinary erotic and even sadistic visions which he then attempts to impose on his readers as an interpretation of the text. Long before that the Victorian Mary Cowden Clarke had written about the girlhood of Shakespeare's heroines in a work more often derided than read. Recent explorations of the sex lives of Shakespeare's mechanicals, like Cowden Clarke's stories, are fantasies released in their author's minds by the texts, but her work, being presented as fiction, not as criticism, has a greater claim to intellectual respectability.

CHAPTER TWO

The originality of Shakespeare's sonnets

This chapter is mainly about Shakespeare's sonnets and their treatment of desire; but as I don't think we can see his sequence clearly without placing it in relation to the sonnet vogue as a whole, and especially in the degree to which he is, on the one hand, subscribing to convention, and on the other hand rebelling against it, I want to begin by sketching the development of the European sonnet tradition and by describing those aspects of contemporary sonnet collections which seem to me to be most interesting in relation to Shakespeare's use of the form. I shall be relying largely, though by no means exclusively, on the reprints of sonnet sequences edited and introduced by Sir Sidney Lee a century ago.[1] Most of the sonnets in Lee's collection date from the 1590s. One can only, rather vaguely, say that they are 'contemporary' with Shakespeare because the dating of his sonnets is a major problem. For this reason, when resemblances exist, it is usually impossible to trace the direction of influence. It may well be significant in attitudes to sexuality that Lee's two volumes do not include the only English sequence to include overtly homoerotic poems, Richard Barnfield's *The Affectionate Shepherd*. After discussing the contemporaries I will go on more directly to a consideration of the originality of Shakespeare's sonnets, and of how this may affect our interpretation of these much discussed poems both poetically and, to a lesser extent, biographically.

The great age of the English sonnet was the last decade of the sixteenth century. Though Shakespeare's sonnets did not appear in print until 1609, we know that he had written some of them ten years before, and at first sight it might seem that he had done so in conformity to a literary fashion. The first great practitioners of the sonnet form were Dante and above all Petrarch, both writing in Italy in the fourteenth century, whose sequences, like those of many of their followers, were interspersed with poems in other metrical and stanzaic forms. Though they had their early followers, including women poets, the vogue they had initiated did not take on international dimensions until the sixteenth century, when sonnet sequences became immensely popular in, especially, Spain, France and England. Sidney Lee, writing a century ago, was able to say that 'One hundred and twenty-one volumes of sonnet-sequences came from Italian presses in the first quarter of the [sixteenth] century; three hundred and twenty-six volumes, most of which bore convincing testimony to the degeneracy of the art, were published during the last quarter.'[2] From Italy the vogue spread to France, where the sonnet was the favoured form of Pierre de Ronsard, Joachim du Bellay and other members of the group of poets known as the Pléiade, often in translation and adaptation from both Italian and classical models, to Spain, and finally to England. Petrarch had been known in England while he still lived: Chaucer refers admiringly to him in the Clerk's Tale, and translates one of his sonnets – though not in sonnet form – in *Troilus and Criseyde*. Then in the early part of the sixteenth century, mainly between 1530 and 1540, Sir Thomas Wyatt translated sonnets by Petrarch and other Italian poets in that 'book of *Songs and Sonnets*', otherwise known as *Tottel's Miscellany*, for which Abraham Slender, in *The Merry Wives of Windsor*, would willingly have paid forty shillings in the hope

that it would assist his wooing of Anne Page (1.1.181–2). The
same volume included sonnets, some of which also were adapted
and even translated from Petrarch, by the Earl of Surrey. The
very first English sonnet sequence is a series of religious sonnets
by the woman poet Anne Lock, published in 1560. In 1582 came
the first collection of love lyrics, *Hecatompathia, or Passionate
Century of Love*, a series of 100 eighteen-line poems by Thomas
Watson which, though not strictly sonnets in the sense most often used today, set a precedent for later sonneteers.[3] (Watson,
incidentally, was later to be accused of murder in coming to
the rescue in a brawl of Marlowe, with whom he was impris-
oned. Thus separate are the achievements of life and art.) It was
not, however, until the late 1580s, with the work of Sir Philip
Sidney, whose *Astrophil and Stella* was published posthumously
in 1591, that the English vogue for collections, or sequences – the
two are not necessarily the same – of sonnets, often interspersed
with poems in other lyric forms, and sometimes followed by a
verse complaint, really took off. During the next seven years at
least nineteen such collections, mostly amorous in subject matter, appeared in print, and several others were written but not
published.[4] Early in the seventeenth century the emphasis shifted
to religious sonnets, and it is not too much to say that by the time
Shakespeare's sonnets were printed, in 1609, the vogue was already out of fashion. This may help to explain why his volume
was not reprinted until 1640, and then in garbled form.

There is no question that Petrarch exerted a colossal influence
on the English sonnet in general, and on Shakespeare in particular, if indirectly. The influence on Shakespeare extends beyond
his own poems in sonnet form to other poems and plays. He refers
directly to the Italian poet in *Romeo and Juliet* when Mercutio,
mocking the lovesick Romeo, says 'Now is he for the numbers

that Petrarch flowed in. Laura' – Petrarch's idealized addressee – compared 'to his lady was a kitchen wench – marry she had a better love to be-rhyme her . . .' (2.3.36–8); and the whole portrayal of Romeo's relationship to the unseen Rosaline mirrors Petrarch's relationship with Laura. Romeo's first encounter with Juliet (1.5.92–105) is cast in the form of a two-handed sonnet, and the entire play is imbued with sonnet conventions in versification, imagery and subject matter.[5] No less conspicuously, in *As You Like It* Orlando's love verses to Rosalind and the portrayal of Silvius's love for Phebe form a joyous but gentle send-up of Petrarchan conventions as filtered through Lodge's *Rosalynde* (Fig. 6).[6]

The fundamental premise of the Petrarchan sonnet is very simple: a man loves and desires a beautiful woman who is dedicated to chastity, which may be either virginity or the 'married chastity' that Shakespeare celebrates in his poem 'The Phoenix and Turtle'. Romeo expresses the idea to Benvolio:

> She'll not be hit
> With Cupid's arrow; she hath Dian's wit,
> And, in strong proof of chastity well armed,
> From love's weak childish bow she lives unharmed.
> She will not stay the siege of loving terms,
> Nor bide th'encounter of assailing eyes,
> Nor ope her lap to saint-seducing gold.
> O, she is rich in beauty, only poor
> That when she dies, with beauty dies her store. (1.1.205–13)

It is only a short step from that to the encouragements to breed in the opening sonnets of Shakespeare's volume. But they are addressed to a man.

Almost all the English sonnet collections of Shakespeare's time are addressed by a man to a woman whom the man idealizes

6. 'Hang there, my verse, in witness of my love': *As You Like It*,
3.2.1: Richard Johnson as Orlando in Glen Byam Shaw's production,
Shakespeare Memorial Theatre, 1957

as Romeo idealizes Rosaline. But as, among the Italian poets, Michelangelo addressed love poems to men, so in England, too, there are just a few exceptions to the general rule in the work of Richard Barnfield, who, interestingly enough, is one of the first writers to mention Shakespeare in print. This is in a poem headed 'A Remembrance of Some English Poets', published in 1598, where he writes:

> And Shakespeare thou, whose honey-flowing vein,
> Pleasing the world, thy praises doth obtain,
> Whose *Venus* and whose *Lucrece* (sweet and chaste)
> Thy name in fame's immortal book have placed:
> > Live ever you, at least in fame live ever:
> > Well may the body die, but fame dies never.

One of Barnfield's longer poems, published in 1594 when he was around twenty years old and written in the same stanza form as *Venus and Adonis*, is 'The Tears of an Affectionate Shepherd Sick for Love; or The Complaint of Daphnis for the Love of Ganymede'. This is sensuously erotic in a manner that far exceeds any of the sonnet sequences addressed to women, more conspicuously resembling Marlowe's homoeroticism in *Hero and Leander* and *Edward II*, which had just been printed. Clearly Barnfield felt a special affinity with Marlowe. In 'The Tears of an Affectionate Shepherd' he quotes an entire line from *Edward II*: writing of 'that fair boy that had my heart entangled' (p. 79, l. 4), Daphnis declares his wish to put 'crownets of pearl about [his] naked arms' (p. 82, l. 104). As Paul Hammond writes, 'Barnfield evidently had a connoisseur's eye for the few homoerotic texts which were available in English, and Marlowe was a frequent source for him.'[7] Probably Barnfield had been keen to buy a copy of *Edward II* hot from the press.

Daphnis addresses Ganymede in lines wide open to homoerotic interpretation:

> O would to God (so I could have my fee)
> My lips were honey, and thy mouth a bee.
> Then shouldst thou suck my sweet and my fair flower
> That now is ripe and full of honey-berries;
> Then would I lead thee to my pleasant bower
> Filled full of grapes, of mulberries, and cherries. (p. 82, ll. 95–100)

And later:

> And every morn by dawning of the day,
> When Phoebus riseth with a blushing face,
> Silvanus' chapel-clerks shall chant a lay,
> And play thee hunts-up in thy resting place:
> > My cot thy chamber, my bosom thy bed,
> > Shall be appointed for thy sleepy head. (p. 82, ll. 109–14)

Interestingly, 'my bosom thy bed' echoes another recently published work concerned with Edward II, Michael Drayton's poem 'Piers Gaveston, Earl of Cornwall'.[8]

The eroticism in Barnfield's poem is pretty explicit, and it seems to have got him into trouble, because in the dedication to his next book, *Cynthia, with Certain Sonnets and the Legend of Cassandra* (1595), he defends himself against the accusation that some 'did interpret *The Affectionate Shepherd* otherwise than as I meant, touching the subject thereof, to wit, the love of a shepherd to a boy'. He claims that his poem was 'nothing else but an imitation of Virgil, in the second Eclogue of Alexis', who writes that 'A shepherd, Corydon, burned with love for his master's favourite, / Handsome Alexis . . .'[9] Well, maybe so; but the new volume includes a sequence of, this time, sonnets also concerned with Ganymede which are explicitly and, it's worth noting, unashamedly and cheerfully homoerotic, full of physical desire:

> Sometimes I wish that I his pillow were,
>   So might I steal a kiss, and yet not seen.
>   So might I gaze upon his sleeping eyne,
> Although I did it with a panting fear;
> But when I well consider how vain my wish is,
>   Ah foolish bees (think I) that do not suck
>   His lips for honey, but poor flowers do pluck
> Which have no sweet in them; when his sole kisses
> Are able to revive a dying soul.
>   Kiss him, but sting him not, for if you do
>   His angry voice your flying will pursue;
> But when they hear his tongue, what can control
>   Their back return? For then they plain may see
>   How honeycombs from his lips dropping be.[10]

The poet's love, we learn, is unrequited; when he confesses that he is in love, his friend assumes that he loves a woman:

> And what is she (quoth he) whom thou dost love?

To which the poet, taking up a covered mirror, responds:

> 'Look in this glass', quoth I, 'there shalt thou see
>   The perfect form of my felicity'.
> When, thinking that it would strange magic prove,
>   He opened it; and taking off the cover
> He straight perceived himself to be my lover.[11] (Fig. 7)

Heterosexual variations on this conceit are to be found elsewhere. In *The Two Gentlemen of Verona*, for example, Silvia persuades Valentine to write a letter ostensibly to a 'secret, nameless friend' of hers who is in fact Valentine himself (2.1.82–158). And in John Webster's tragedy *The Duchess of Malfi* (1614), the

7. Crispin van den Broeck, *Two Young Men with an Apple*

Duchess reveals her love to Antonio by a more sophisticated version of the device.

Barnfield's sonnets are exceptional not only in being addressed to a man but in the explicitness of their expressions of desire. Almost all the male to female sequences of the 1590s are, in spite of their expressions of desire, chaste in the way in which they formulate it. There are, admittedly, occasional lines that might be misinterpreted; I rather cherish a couple from one of the less distinguished sequences, William Percy's *Coelia*, where, imagining that his mistress has recoiled from touching him with her foot, he asks 'What! Do you jerk it off so nimbly, / As though, in very sooth, a snake had bit it!'[12] And Barnabe Barnes, in his *Parthenophil and Parthenophe*, has a conceit that is more obscene than erotic; imagining himself, in the familiar fashion,

to be various objects associated with his mistress, he wishes that
he might fold her pearl necklace

> About that lovely neck, and her paps tickle!
>> Or her to compass, like a belt of gold!
> Or that sweet wine, which down her throat doth trickle,
>> To kiss her lips, and lie next at her heart,
>> Run through her veins, and pass by pleasure's part![13]

Sidney Lee found the allusion to 'pleasure's part' so objection-
able that, censuring Barnes for conceits that are 'grotesque' – as
is fair enough – and 'offensive' – which is a matter of taste – he
quoted in his Introduction only the first line of the couplet: 'To
kiss her lips, and lie next at her heart' – though he would have
made his point better by including the final line – 'Run through
her veins, and pass by pleasure's part!' (Introduction, p. lxxv).
The overall chastity of expression in sonnet sequences other
than Shakespeare's extends even, for instance, to Michael
Drayton's *Idea* which, written over more than twenty-five years,
implies a successful relationship without using explicitly sexual
imagery.

Drayton is deeply indebted to continental models, and in this
he resembles most sonneteers of the period. The idea that the av-
erage sonneteer looked in his heart and wrote, as Sidney's Muse
bade him do,[14] could not be further from the truth. Lee, writing of
the 'wholesale loans which the Elizabethan sonneteers invariably
levied on foreign literature', remarks that 'genuine originality of
thought and expression was rare'. Some of them, he continues,
'prove, when their work is compared with that of foreign writers,
to have been verbatim translators, and almost sink to the level
of literary pirates'.[15] Giles Fletcher's *Licia*, published in 1593,
at least has the honesty to announce on its title page that these
'poems of love in honour of the admirable and singular virtues of

his Lady', as he calls them, so far from being personal outpour-
ings, are written in 'imitation of the best Latin Poets and others'.
Licia, he teasingly writes, may be a mere abstraction, perhaps
'Learning's Image, or some heavenly wonder . . . perhaps under
that name I have shadowed "[The Holy] Discipline"', or perhaps 'that kind courtesy which I found at the Patroness of these
Poems', or 'some College' (he had been a Fellow of King's College, Cambridge), or 'It may be my conceit and pretend nothing.'
'A man may write of love and not be in love, as well as of hus-
bandry and not go to the plough, or of witches and be none, or of
holiness and be flat profane.'[16] Is this deliberate obfuscation, we
may ask, a playful attempt to deflect enquiry into a living object
of love? The depth of Giles Fletcher's indebtedness to continental and other models suggests not: suggests in fact that his
sonnets are, as Shakespeare's have often been described, literary
exercises largely divorced from personal experience.

Is that true of Shakespeare's sonnets too? Do they proceed
from real-life situations reflecting his own personal experience
or are they fictionally crafted? – though even if they are they
must still derive ultimately from personal emotional experience.
A few of them are meditations with no immediate relevance to
day-to-day reality. But most of them give at least the appearance
of emerging from a series of real-life events. Comparison with
other sequences can help us here. In his plays, Shakespeare is
an extraordinarily literary writer, constantly drawing on a wide
range of printed and even manuscript sources. Yet the sonnets
are quite exceptional in their relationship to other sequences
in their lack of derivativeness. They occasionally reflect their
author's reading in, for instance, Ovid, Erasmus and – most
conspicuously but in two of the slightest and least apparently
personal of the sonnets, Nos. 153 and 154 – the *Greek Anthology*.

But they show none of that dependence on continental models which is so conspicuous a feature of the other sequences.[17] As we have seen, if they reflect earlier writings it appears to be by reaction against them rather than in imitation of them. The very fact that the story they tell is obscure argues for their basis in reality: Shakespeare could surely have done better than this if he had been trying to imply a coherent narrative. Some of the sonnets are inward-looking, with allusions that seem intended for one pair of eyes alone. I think not simply of references to absence, to infidelity, to rivalry, to difference of age, to feelings of inferiority, which might seem particular but could easily be part of a fictional scenario, but rather of lines like

> Were't aught to me I bore the canopy,
> With my extern the outward honouring,
> Or laid great bases for eternity
> Which proves more short than waste or ruining?
> (Sonnet 125, ll. 1–4)

That reads to me more like a private allusion than anything that a general reader could ever have been expected to understand.

The circumstances of the publication of the sonnets also seem relevant. If Shakespeare was writing as a public poet, for money – as he was in the narrative poems – he would surely have published his poems himself, and would probably have done so at a time when the sonnet vogue was still fashionable enough for him to have made a success with them. Instead they were clearly a flop on their first appearance. Shakespeare was a dramatist who could speak for people far different from himself, as we see from the vast range of characters in his plays. If he could write to order the anguished speeches of, say, Angelo, in *Measure for Measure*, or of Hamlet or Othello in their most passionate moments, he could also have written poems on the basis of imagined rather than actual experience.

As a scholar, I have to admit this. But if I were required to jump over the fence rather than sit on it, I should have to come out with the view that many of the sonnets, including – indeed, especially – those that seem most revelatory of sexual infatuation and self-disgust, are private poems, personal and almost confessional in nature, like the erotic drawings of Henry Fuseli, J. M. W. Turner or Duncan Grant.

One other feature that most other sequences have in common which is relevant to comparison with Shakespeare is that they are indeed sequences: unified collections of poems linked by a common addressee, by formal links from one poem to another which may extend to their making up a 'corona', that is, a collection of poems designed to be read in sequence in which the whole or part of the last line of one becomes the first of the next, and the last poem returns to the first.

Shakespeare's sonnets are obviously not a unified sequence in this or any other sense. But nor are they a totally random assemblage of diverse poems. Made up of 154 poems and thus easily the longest collection of the period, they have, exceptionally, at least two addressees. They do not name any of their recipients except by implication in those that pun on the name 'Will' (Nos. 135, 136, and possibly 57 and 143) – a far cry from the etherealized Dianas and Zepherias, Diellas and Lauras of other collections. Some of them are meditations with little, if any, relevance to the main sequence: for instance, the profound, though damaged No. 146, beginning 'Poor soul, the centre of my sinful earth', would be perfectly at home in a religious sequence.

Though the collection as a whole has no unity, it is possible to identify mini-sequences within it, most obviously the first seventeen sonnets, with their repeated adjunctions to a young man to marry and to breed. Some pairs are linked in subject matter, some form double sonnets, and all the poems that are unquestionably addressed to a woman are placed at the end, though they do not have the thematic and stylistic unity of the first seventeen poems. It is sometimes said that the story the sonnets tell – in so far as they tell a story at all, because considered as a piece of story-telling they are, not to put too fine a point upon it, crap – covers a period of three years; but this theory is blown sky high if, as seems likely, No. 145, with its puns on 'hate' and 'away', is a relic of Shakespeare's courtship of Anne Hathaway, completed by 1581.[18] Irregular in form, it is composed in octosyllabics.

If the collection could include one poem written early in Shakespeare's career, it could include others written at any point until the volume went to press. In his plays, Shakespeare makes most use of the sonnet form in, for instance, *Love's Labour's Lost* and, above all, *Romeo and Juliet*, written we believe around 1594 to 1595, and it is often assumed that the bulk of his independent sonnets were composed around then, when the sonnet vogue was at its height. On the other hand, the epilogue to *Henry V*, of 1599, is in sonnet form. So is the letter that Helen writes to the Countess in *All's Well that Ends Well* (3.4.4–17) of around 1603, and still later, in *Cymbeline* (c. 1610), Jupiter speaks an extended sonnet (5.5.186–207).

The first external evidence of sonnets by Shakespeare comes from 1598, when Francis Meres, in his book *Palladis Tamia*, wrote of his 'sugared sonnets among his private friends' – and perhaps we should remember that the term 'sonnet' was highly flexible, not necessarily referring to the 'quatorzain' by which the form was alternatively known. None of John Donne's *Songs and*

Sonnets, for instance, is a fourteen-liner. Manuscript circulation was common, though Meres's allusion – 'sugared sonnets among his private friends' – might imply that Shakespeare was keen to keep his sonnets away from the public eye, for whatever reason. Versions of two of them – Nos. 138 and 144 – appeared without authority, presumably from privately circulated manuscripts, in *The Passionate Pilgrim* of 1599. It has recently been argued that rather than being, as had previously been supposed, debased versions they are in fact early versions later revised.[19] This would support the possibility that the whole collection as printed in 1609 was consciously put together and revised by Shakespeare himself from pre-existing poems at some undetermined date before then. Some of them include cryptic allusions that could refer to date-able events, but none of them has been finally pinned down to a specific date. One sonnet, No. 107, known somewhat laughably as the 'dating sonnet', with its reference to 'the mortal moon' that 'hath her eclipse endured', has been variously taken to refer to the Armada of 1588, to Queen Elizabeth's having survived her Grand Climacteric – her sixty-third year, 1595–6 – and, perhaps most plausibly, to the death of Elizabeth followed by the accession of James I in 1603. The possibility that Shakespeare himself put the sonnets into the order in which they were printed is enhanced if we accept the hypothesis that the numbering of some of them is significant – No. 12, for example, with its reference to 'the clock that tells the time', and No. 60, in which the poet writes that 'our minutes hasten to their end'. It seems certain to me that, though some of the sonnets may have been written in groups within a relatively short period, the collection as a whole gathers together poems written over a long period of time – perhaps as much as twenty-five years – and rearranges them in a sequence that only fitfully reflects their order of composition.

Although Shakespeare was undoubtedly influenced by Petrarchism, his sequence departs from its conventions in many significant ways. Most conspicuous of all is the fact that, as I have said, many of the poems, like some of Barnfield's but none, so far as I know, by any other sonneteer of the period, are explicitly addressed to, or concern, a man. Evidence for this lies in forms of address, such as 'Lord of my love' (No. 26), 'sweet boy' (No. 108), 'lovely boy' (No. 126), and personal pronouns. By my reckoning thirty of the poems, all among the first 126, are indisputably addressed to, or primarily concern, a man; thirteen are clearly about a woman (the 'dark lady'), and these are all in the later part of the collection, from No. 127 onwards. One, No. 144 – 'Two loves I have, of comfort and despair' – shows the poet torn between a man and a woman. All the remainder (excluding No. 146) could have either a male or a female as their topic, though up to No. 126 context suggests a male. Yet some of the poems which, judging by their place within the collection, are written to a man are regularly anthologized as gender-free love poems: 'Shall I compare thee to a summer's day?' (No. 18), addressed by many a lad to his lass, may seem more likely from its place in the sequence to be addressed to the fair (which may mean simply 'attractive' or 'beautiful') friend (which may mean 'lover'); so may 'Let me not to the marriage of true minds' (No. 116), frequently read at heterosexual marriages. It is unclear whether there is more than one friend. In what follows I shall at times, for convenience, speak of the young man, but with the proviso that he need not be the same throughout. And as I have said, the only name that emerges is Shakespeare's own, Will, relentlessly and bawdily punned upon in some of the later sonnets.

The first seventeen of the sonnets as printed read as if they might be the first to be written to the/a young man in that they are both more formal in terms of address and more uniform in subject matter than the later sonnets. They do not at first imply a loving relationship, though, in urging a man to marry and have children, the poet feels intimate enough with his friend to criticise him for masturbating when he could be having heterosexual intercourse: in the very first poem the 'tender churl' is said to bury his content 'within his own bud', and in No. 4 to have 'traffic with [himself] alone'. It is the poet's perception and admiration of the young man's beauty that motivate his urgings; he is confident enough of the friend's affections to ask him to 'make thee another self *for love of me*' (No. 10), in No. 13 he addresses him as 'love' and 'dear my love', and in No. 15 (part of a double sonnet) he is 'all in war with time for love of you'.

Many of the sonnets in the first part – such as No. 17, 'Who will believe my verse in time to come / If it were filled with your most high deserts?' – idealize their beloved in the Petrarchan fashion – and this one is definitely addressed to a man; none of those in the second part, clearly addressed to a woman, do. On the other hand, most of the sonnets even in the first part are written, as it were, from within an existing relationship. The beloved is not, in Petrarchan fashion, a remote figure to be adored from afar. In many poems the poet's love is reciprocated: his heart 'lives' in his friend's, he can say 'Presume not on thy heart when mine is slain: / Thou gav'st me thine not to give back again' (this is No. 22). Still, the young man – if there is only one – is not perfect; as Michael Spiller, author of an excellent study called *The Development of the Sonnet*, writes, 'for the first time in the entire history of the sonnet, the desired object is *flawed*'.[20] The linked sonnets Nos. 40 to 42 imply that their subject has committed sexual infidelity with the poet's mistress – and therefore incidentally provide evidence for the simultaneity of events in the two parts of the collection – and No. 42, a poem which exquisitely explores the complexity of the poet's emotions, states clearly that the loss of the man 'touches [the poet] more nearly' than the woman's infidelity. In the couplet, the poet declares that 'here's the joy: my friend and I are one. / Sweet flattery! Then she loves but me alone.'

If the young man involved in a triangular relationship with the poet and the woman – and the dedication's reference to 'the only begetter of these ensuing sonnets' supports the assumption that this man is the same throughout – is open to, and receives, criticism, the woman – again we must make the qualification that there might be more than one woman, but this seems less likely than with the man – is positively reviled. The first part of the collection ends with a poem, No. 126, addressed to 'my lovely boy'; the second part begins with one concerned with – though not addressed to – the poet's mistress whose 'eyes are raven-black, / Her brow so suited'. Is she black in skin, as Margreta de Grazia, among others, has argued?[21] Unlikely I think – brow commonly meant 'eyebrow'. There is no doubt that the poet is in love with the woman, but O!, how he wishes he were not. A few of the poems express affection and admiration; they include the playful No. 128 – 'How oft when thou, my music, music play'st' – though this is not gender-specific and could relate to a man even though it's in the second part – and the anti-Petrarchan send-up 'My mistress' eyes are nothing like the sun', which, for all its jokiness, concludes

> And yet, by heaven, I think my love as rare
> As any she belied with false compare. (Sonnet 130)

But in other poems the poet unmercifully castigates himself for his folly in being emotionally entangled with a woman for whom he can feel no respect. Although to his 'dear doting heart' she is 'the fairest and most precious jewel', in the same poem she is 'tyrannous' and 'black' in her 'deeds' (No. 131); her eyes 'torment' him 'with disdain'; in a sonnet clearly related to No. 41 he curses her for the 'deep wound' that her heart gives to 'my friend and me', claiming that the woman has caused him to be forsaken 'of him, myself, and thee', and in the linked subsequent sonnet he offers, in an elaborately metaphysical conceit, to give up himself provided that she restores his friend 'to be my comfort still'.

These extraordinarily agonized and agonizing poems (one is reminded of Catullus's 'Odi et amo' – 'I love and I hate') reveal – or create the sense of – a man who is and remains as deeply entangled emotionally with the man as with the woman. These surely are poems in which the poet is talking to himself, trying to work through and to gain control over an emotional crisis by imposing poetic form upon an expression of feelings that no words can ultimately assuage. Some of them parallel the self-torment of a Hamlet or an Angelo – or, in a later period and different context, of Gerard Manley Hopkins. It is hard to imagine them being shown to their addressee. In the sonnets that pun on the word 'will', playfulness becomes bitter and self-lacerating. And some of the poems use sexually suggestive language in a manner that is unparalleled in any other sonnet collection of this or, perhaps, any other period. As in the plays, there are times when an image touched on only in passing soon afterwards becomes the centre of a complex nexus of associations in a way that may suggest continuity of composition. So in No. 134 the poet declares himself 'mortgaged to' the woman's 'will', and then in No. 135 we have a dazzling torrent of wordplay on the word 'will' in various senses including the poet's name (which may also be that of the friend who is his rival for the woman's favours), 'testament', 'wish', '(sexual) desire', and both the male – modern 'willy' – and female sexual organs.

> Whoever hath her wish, thou hast thy Will,
> And Will to boot, and Will in overplus.
> More than enough am I that vex thee still,
> To thy sweet will making addition thus.
> Wilt thou, whose will is large and spacious,
> Not once vouchsafe to hide my will in thine?
> Shall will in others seem right gracious,
> And in my will no fair acceptance shine?
> The sea, all water, yet receives rain still,
> And in abundance addeth to his store;
> So thou, being rich in Will, add to thy Will
> One will of mine to make thy large Will more.
>   Let no unkind no fair beseechers kill;
>   Think all but one, and me in that one Will. (Sonnet 135)

The serious use of cumulative sexual innuendo here – 'thou, whose will is large and spacious', 'vouchsafe to hide my will in thine' – is as powerful as anything in the language of Hamlet or Iago, Leontes or Posthumus. The woman is accused, not merely of infidelity with the friend, but of whorish promiscuity: though the poet's eyes 'know what beauty is' – which I take to refer to the young man's beauty – they are so corrupted by the woman's looks as to 'Be anchored in the bay where all men ride', falsifying his judgement to the point where he 'think[s] that a several plot' (i.e. a bodily part dedicated solely to him) while knowing in his heart that it is 'the wide world's common place' (No. 137). The triangularity reaches a climax in the great sonnet beginning 'Two loves I have, of comfort and despair' – greater poetry, perhaps, than some of the more anguished sonnets because in it the poet seems to have reached enough of a resolution of his torments to be able to write about them with relative dispassion

8. 'Two loves I have, of comfort and despair' (Sonnet 144):
Christopher Gable, Rudolf Nureyev and Lynn Seymour in the ballet
Images of Love by Kenneth MacMillan, Royal Opera House, London,
1964

in a kind of miniature morality play (Fig. 8):

> Two loves I have, of comfort and despair,
> Which like two spirits do suggest me still.
> The better angel is a man right fair,
> The worser spirit a woman coloured ill.

To win me soon to hell my female evil
Tempteth my better angel from my side,
And would corrupt my saint to be a devil,
Wooing his purity with her foul pride;
And whether that my angel be turned fiend
Suspect I may, yet not directly tell;
But being both from me, both to each friend,
I guess one angel in another's hell.
    Yet this shall I ne'er know, but live in doubt
    Till my bad angel fire my good one out. (Sonnet 144)

It's a kind of serious version of Lancelot Gobbo's parable of the conscience and the devil in *The Merchant of Venice* (2.2.1–29). Its formal perfection may suggest self-control, but the depth of the poet's feelings is conveyed with bitter intensity in the wordplay on both 'angel' and 'hell' in the sense of sexual organ, and in the implication of venereal disease in the word 'fire'.

The unique and blatant sexuality of the poems reaches its climax in the extreme contrast between soul and body in No. 151:

thou betraying me, I do betray
My nobler part to my gross body's treason.
My soul doth tell my body that he may
Triumph in love; flesh stays no farther reason,
But rising at thy name doth point out thee
As his triumphant prize. Proud of this pride,
He is contented thy poor drudge to be,
To stand in thy affairs, fall by thy side.
    No want of conscience hold it that I call
    Her 'love' for whose dear love I rise and fall.

Even if we find Helen Vendler's belief that this poem's use of the words 'conscience' and 'contented' involves wordplay on 'cunt'[22] an example of lewd interpretation, as I do, the sustained and undisguised phallic imagery of erection, orgasm and detumescence in those lines is the ultimate reversal of Petrarchism. This is an unashamedly sexual lover glorying with lewd explicitness in his ability to satisfy his and his woman's physical desires even as he admits its 'gross'-ness.

In the second group of sonnets, those addressed to one or more women, a sexual relationship is beyond question. The notion that such a relationship between men is implied in the earlier group was for long anathema to admirers of Shakespeare. The first time the sonnets were reprinted, by John Benson in 1640, thirty-one years after they had first appeared, pronouns in three of them were altered from male to female, as if in deference to the requirements of decorum, and eight of them, including two explicitly addressed to a male, were omitted. Many of the remainder were run together to form seventy-two poems in all, and they were given titles suggestive of heterosexual romance (No. 8, 'Music to hear . . .' becomes 'An Invitation to Marriage', and No. 113, 'Since I left you . . .', 'Self-flattery of her Beauty').

From Malone (writing in 1790) onwards, commentators have felt obliged to invoke Renaissance notions of male friendship as a way of explaining that, as Hyder Rollins[23] puts it, 'in the Elizabethan period men often addressed one another in loving terms which to the Georgians sounded indecorous', and thus of denying a physical element in the poet's relationship with his friend(s). George Chalmers, reacting to his enemy Malone, proposed in 1797 that the sonnets were addressed to Queen Elizabeth, explaining that she was often thought of as a man.[24] So 'Shakespeare's admirers' may be reassured that 'the poet was incapable of such grossness' as to write sonnets 'professing too much love to be addressed to a man'. It is too much to assume 'that Shakespeare, a moral man, addressed a hundred and twenty, nay, a hundred and twenty-six *Amourous* [sic] Sonnets to a *male* object!' Chalmers's efforts to substantiate his case in relation to the 'prick' of Sonnet 20 lead him to extremes of ingenuity. Refuting suggestions that it is 'too *indecent* to be quoted', he writes that 'It is for impure minds only, to be continually finding something obscene in objects, that convey nothing obscene, or offensive, to the chastest hearts.'[25] Coleridge, assuring his son Hartley that in all Shakespeare's 'numerous plays' 'there is not even an allusion to that very worst of all possible vices', defended '[Shakespeare's] "pure love" for the young man of the sonnets'. 'O my son!' he concludes, 'I pray fervently that thou may'st know inwardly how impossible it was for a Shakespere not to have been in his heart's heart chaste.'[26] Much later in the nineteenth century Oscar Wilde, in his novella *Portrait of Mr W. H.*, first published in 1889 and later revised, caused his central character to explain the language in which Shakespeare addressed, as he surmised, the boy player Willie Hughes as a symptom of neo-Platonism: 'There was a kind of mystic transference of the expressions of the physical sphere to a sphere that was spiritual, that was removed from gross bodily appetite, and in which the soul was Lord.'[27] But Wilde may have had his tongue in his cheek when he invented the theory that Marlowe stole the boy from Shakespeare so that the lad could play the role of Edward II's lover Gaveston in his play *Edward II*. And at least one writer of this period was willing to admit his belief that 'the love of the English poet for Mr W H was, though only for a short time, more Greek than English'.[28] Those are the words of Samuel Butler, author of *Erewhon* and *The Way of All Flesh*, who was one of the sonnets' greatest all-time admirers. At the beginning of his book *Shakespeare's Sonnets Reconsidered*, of 1899, he tells us that he committed all of them to memory within a few months, and that after that he had 'daily from that time repeated twenty-five of them, to complete the process of saturation'.[29]

For all the denials, there is no question that many of the later sonnets addressed to and concerned with a young man indicate a highly charged emotional relationship in which a psychologist might well identify a homoerotic element that might or might not be recognized by either or both of the men. Sonnet 20 has become a battleground in discussions of the relationship. On the surface it offers an explicit denial of a sexual element in the relationship between the poet and his friend:

> . . . for a woman wert thou first created,
> Till nature as she wrought thee fell a-doting,
> And by addition me of thee defeated
> By adding one thing to my purpose nothing.
>> But since she pricked thee out for woman's pleasure,
>> Mine be thy love and thy love's use their treasure. (Fig. 9)

The overtness of the sexual reference is part of Shakespeare's originality evidenced in many other aspects of the sonnets. A critic has written that

> The sonnet reveals a man who is nearly obsessed by the fact
> that his lover has a penis. By expressing this awareness on
> paper, he has violated all the decorum proper to the missives
> between a faithful friend and his alter ipse. I can find no other
> example in Renaissance literature, either in England or on the
> continent, in which a gentleman even hints at, much less so
> blatantly, his friend's genital endowment and its relation to his
> own pleasure. The tacky dismissal of its usefulness to him
> raises an issue that should otherwise have gone unnoticed.[30]

Ostensibly the lines mean that the poet has no use for the other man's sexual parts – his 'thing' (a common euphemism for the penis, played on, for example, by Viola disguised as a boy in *Twelfth Night* – 'a little thing would make me tell them how much I lack of a man' (3.4.293–4)). Even in recent writings this

9. 'The master-mistress of my passion' (Sonnet 20). This portrait, attributed to John de Critz (c. 1551/2–1642) or his workshop, of Shakespeare's patron Henry Wriothesley, third Earl of Southampton, as a late-teenager was thought until 2002 to be of a woman, Lady Norton

explanation is sometimes accepted: Spiller, for instance, writes 'Shakespeare's love for the young man was not physically homosexual, as Sonnet 20 makes quite clear.'[31] But at least since the 1960s reasons have been brought forward to argue that this sonnet does not deny the possibility of a sexual relationship. Stephen Orgel, working from the original Quarto spelling, without apostrophes, argues that 'the "women's pleasure" the friend is "pricked out for" (i.e. selected for . . .) is not the pleasure he gives women but his ability to take pleasure as women do; "loves" in the last line is then not a possessive but a plural, and "use" is a verb – the line without its modern apostrophe need not be a renunciation at all: "let my love be yours, and let your loves make use of their treasure".'[32] I confess to finding it hard to get my mind round this explanation. But even if the couplet is taken at face value, this sonnet is placed early in the sequence – relationships alter with the passage of time. And in any case the young man addressed in this poem is not necessarily the same as the one addressed in others, with whom the poet may have had a totally different relationship. And whatever the poet says about this young man's prick, the earlier part of the poem shows that he finds the rest of the young man as attractive as he might expect himself to find a woman whom he might desire:

> A woman's face with nature's own hand painted
> Hast thou, the master-mistress of my passion;
> A woman's gentle heart, but not acquainted
> With shifting change as is false women's fashion . . .

There is also a touch of misogyny here – 'false women's fashion' – as in other sonnets of the earlier group, which prefigures the revulsion against female sexuality in the sonnets addressed to the woman, and in some of the plays, most noticeably *King Lear* and *Timon of Athens*. The New Penguin editor, John Kerrigan, with I suspect a touch of irony, remarks that while some interpreters treat the words 'master-mistress of my passion' as a joke – 'you, . . . like the conventional sonnet mistress, are nevertheless male' – other critics, 'of coarser fibre, prefer "you, the seductively androgynous object of my homosexual lust"'.[33] Is it significant that this is the only poem in the collection to use feminine rhymes throughout?

None of Shakespeare's poems is as explicitly homoerotic as any of Barnfield's. Yet Shakespeare's are more intense in their expressions of love – which could be simply because Shakespeare was the greater poet. His poems use the language of love: 'Lord of my love' (No. 26), 'my friend and I are one' (No. 42), 'thou mine, I thine', 'eternal love' (No. 108), 'my lovely boy' (No. 126). Though this may have been the conventional language of non-sexual friendship, it was certainly also the language of sexual love. Many of the poems are drenched in the language of longing and desire, of sadness in absence and joy at thoughts of the friend's 'sweet love' (No. 29), speaking of sleepless nights during which the poet's thoughts make 'a zealous pilgrimage' to the beloved (Nos. 27, 61), of mutual possession and shared identity (Nos. 31, 36, 39), of the poet as 'slave' to his friend's 'desire' (No. 57; according to Michael Spiller, the word 'had a narrower meaning than today, denoting sexual appetite'[34]), of fears of loss (No. 64), of dependency (No. 75, 'So are you to my thoughts as food to life'). It would be a naive young man who, addressed in these terms, did not regard himself as the object of desire. If Shakespeare himself did not, in the fullest sense of the word, love a man, he certainly understood the feelings of those who do.

CHAPTER THREE

'I think he loves the world only for him': men loving men in Shakespeare's plays

In writing about sexuality in Shakespeare's sonnets I distin-guished between explicit and implicit meanings – those that are clear from the text, such as the fact that the poet had sexual re-lations with the woman, and those that have to be extrapolated from the text, such as whether he had sexual relations with the (or a) 'sweet boy'. In this chapter I want to turn to the plays, doc-uments that by their very nature are even more conspicuously open to interpretation than poems. I shall discuss some of the ways in which plays may be interpreted, or even appropriated, by reading within or beneath the lines in a manner that may not necessarily contradict their tenor, may even reinforce hints contained in the lines, but could also be said to go against the plays' explicit meanings to mirror the preoccupations of their in-terpreters – as has often been said of homoerotic readings of the sonnets. Specifically, I want to talk about homosexual interpreta-tions, on both page and stage, of male characters in Shakespeare.

This is not, of course, the only way in which Shakespeare's plays can be appropriated. It would be possible, for example, to discuss ways in which the political preoccupations of various ages have been reflected in criticism and performance. In such instances, however, it can be clearly said that interpretation is the result of interaction between the text and events of a time differ-ent from that in which it was composed. It may be interesting and effective to relate *Richard III* to the rise of Nazism, as in Richard

Eyre's 1990 National Theatre production (and the film of 1995 based on it and directed by Richard Loncraine) through costume and other production devices. It may be fascinating to overlay *Hamlet* with images of Communist Romania and the Ceausescus, as in a Romanian production of 1989, and to see how the tenor reacts with the vehicle, but no one could claim that the latter-day significances had been available to Shakespeare as he wrote, or to early audiences as they saw the plays performed. But the areas of psychological subtext, of personal and specifically sexual relationships in the plays that I shall discuss, are less tied down to local and temporal circumstances. They offer a subtler challenge because although they may reflect twentieth-century preoccupations, we cannot claim in any absolute sense of many of them that they represent impositions upon the plays. It would be no less possible to say that they draw up meanings from the plays' – perhaps from Shakespeare's – subconscious, that they actualize that which is latent in the lines, and do so in a manner that must always be open to a performer – or, for that matter, to any interpreter. If the plays are open to gay readings then those readings have their own kind of validity.

Let us take a well-known example that does not apply to my principal topic. At the end of *Measure for Measure* the Duke twice proposes marriage to Isabella. Before this advanced stage in the play's action they have more than once been seen together in circumstances of some intimacy. There has been no verbal hint of any developing amatory relationship, but given the revelation in the final scene that by this point in the play the Duke seeks marriage to Isabella, it would be entirely natural, even in a production in which Isabella does not respond favourably to the Duke's proposal, for the actor playing the Duke to read back into the play's earlier scenes the information that he will give at its close, and to seek to convey to the audience that he is falling in love with Isabella some time before he makes his first verbal declaration. This lies within the normal bounds of theatrical interpretation and could have happened in Shakespeare's company as well as in later ones.

The implied relationship between the Duke and Isabella is of course heterosexual in nature, and Shakespeare's plays are full of such relationships that are made fully explicit in the text. Many of his plays are concerned with courtship and marriage, many culminate in the successful outcome of heterosexual courtship with full verbal acknowledgement of sexuality. 'Come, Kate, we'll to bed', says Petruccio (*The Taming of the Shrew*, 5.2.189); 'Sweet friends, to bed', says Theseus (*A Midsummer Night's Dream*, 5.1.361). Shakespeare is the greatest celebrant of heterosexual love.

His plays are full, too, of friendship between members of the same sex, affectionate, even loving relationships in which there is nevertheless no explicit declaration or other manifestation of sexual interest. Whereas, to take a very obvious example, it is perfectly clear in Marlowe's play *Edward II* that Edward and Gaveston are lovers, it is not easy in Shakespeare's plays to point to the portrayal of any same-sex relationships that are of a sexual nature, or to identify more than a very few indubitable references to homosexual behaviour or relationships.

The topic was treated in a pioneering fashion by Eric Partridge in his essay 'The Sexual: the Homosexual: and Non-Sexual Bawdy in Shakespeare' which forms the introduction to *Shakespeare's Bawdy*. Partridge writes: 'The definite references to male homosexuality are few. Perhaps the clearest cut passages are these two: "*Thersites*. Thou art thought to be Achilles' male varlet! – *Patroclus*. Male varlet, you rogue, what's that? – *Thersites*. Why, his masculine whore." [*Troilus and Cressida*, 5.1.15–17] . . . and the Hostess, concerning Falstaff, says "In good faith, 'a cares not what mischief he doth, if his weapon be out: he will foin like any devil; he will spare neither man, woman, nor child"' (*Henry IV*, Part Two, 2.1.15–18).[1] The first of these instances is absolutely explicit in its use of the phrases 'male varlet' and 'masculine whore'. The second, though difficult to deny, depends upon wordplay; weapon and foin (meaning thrust) have innocent senses as well as bawdy ones. And as soon as one admits innuendo in words of doubtful meaning, or in secondary senses of words that have an innocent primary meaning, one opens the way to a great deal more allusiveness than Partridge acknowledges. For instance, in *All's Well that Ends Well*, the young Count Bertram, speaking of the disreputable Paroles after his exposure, says of him 'I could endure anything before but a cat, and now he's a cat to me' (4.3.242–3). The word 'cat' here seems to have some special meaning, and it has been conjectured that it means 'catamite' used insultingly – whether or not literally – of Paroles. Partridge appears not to have thought of this but it is mentioned in Frankie Rubinstein's *Dictionary of Shakespeare's Sexual Puns and their Significance* (under 'both-sides'), and is not inconsistent with what we know of Paroles,[2] though at the same time it is not supported by anything else in the play.[3]

Since Partridge's time bawdy interpretations of Shakespeare have grown apace, and many of them impute homosexual significance to passages in which it had not been found before. And it is not necessary to be a highly experienced playgoer to have seen productions of his plays in which homosexuality is made explicit.

In my first chapter I referred to arguments about whether Cleopatra's words, 'Husband, I come', might bear a sexual interpretation. It would be an understatement to say that no one doubts Cleopatra's heterosexuality. To that extent the possibility of wordplay in these words opens up no new revelations about her character. But the identification of similar wordplay concerning relationships between men might have a profound effect on our view of a character's sexual orientation, and thus alter our interpretation of a play. Indeed, such an effect may be created not by wordplay in the ordinary sense, by bawdy or innuendo, but by the admission of significances to words used in one situation that they might naturally have in another.

We are, I take it, conditioned to suppose that more than merely conventional expressions of affection between persons of the opposite sex imply the possibility of a sexual relationship. We are, or at least we have until recently been, equally conditioned to suppose that even quite intense expressions of affection between men may imply no such possibility. And in works of the past we are accustomed to a conditioned denial to a whole range of words when used between men of significances that we should automatically ascribe to them when used of or between men and women.

Let us take a few examples. 'Come what may, I do adore thee so / That danger shall seem sport, and I will go.' That is the sea captain Antonio of Sebastian, in *Twelfth Night* (2.1.42–3). In the first scene of *The Two Gentlemen of Verona*, Valentine addresses his friend Proteus as 'my loving Proteus' and Proteus responds with 'Sweet Valentine'. Later Valentine addresses 'Sweet Proteus' (1.1.1,11,56). In *Coriolanus*, Aufidius says to Coriolanus

> Let me twine
> Mine arms about that body whereagainst
> My grainèd ash an hundred times hath broke,
> And scarred the moon with splinters.
> *He embraces Coriolanus*
> Here I clip

The anvil of my sword, and do contest
As hotly and as nobly with thy love
As ever in ambitious strength I did
Contend against thy valour. Know thou first,
I loved the maid I married, never man
Sighed truer breath. But that I see thee here,
Thou noble thing, more dances my rapt heart
Than when I first my wedded mistress saw
Bestride my threshold. (4.5.107–19)

In modern plays such language would almost inevitably carry along with it imputations of homosexuality. But in Shakespeare, by an exercise of the historical sense, out of a feeling that this must be how chaps talked to one another in those days, and anyway that this is poetry and so not to be judged by normal standards of common sense, we suppress any such reaction.

Or at least we used to. When did we stop repressing our natural reactions to words in these circumstances? – or, if you like, when did we start allowing the possibilities of sexual undertones to rise to the surface? I have come across no homosexual reading of any of Shakespeare's plays in the first three hundred years of their existence. Such readings did not start, so far as I can tell, until the late nineteenth century, by which time, as I have said, the possibility that Shakespeare himself had sexual relationships with men was being quite widely and openly discussed.

The later part of the nineteenth century was, I take it, a particularly significant period in the history of attitudes to sexuality. Michel Foucault dates the birth of what he calls 'the psychological, psychiatric, medical category of homosexuality' from 1870, with the publication of an article by Carl Westphal 'on contrary sexual sensations'.[4] It's a bit like C. S. Lewis's dating, in *The Allegory of Love* (1936), of the beginnings of romantic love to the

eleventh century, or Philip Larkin's 'Sexual intercourse began /
In nineteen sixty-three, / (which was rather late for me) – /
Between the end of the "Chatterley" ban / And the Beatles'
first LP.'[5]

England seems to have hung behind the Continent. It was not
until 1885 that the Criminal Law Amendment Act formulated
punishments for sodomy and for what were described as acts 'of
gross indecency' which were to be inflicted upon Oscar Wilde
ten years later. A number of books, such as A. J. Symonds's *A
Problem in Modern Ethics* (1891) and Edward Carpenter's *Ho-
mogenic Love* (1894), idealized homosexuality; Havelock Ellis's
Sexual Inversion of 1897 was a scientific study, and Krafft-Ebing's
Psychopathia Sexualis appeared in 1899, the year in which, as we
have seen, the bisexual Samuel Butler described Shakespeare
as 'Greek' in his love for Mr W. H.[6] Since then the debate has
shown no signs of abating. A detailed study of the sonnets published in 1985 presents them as 'the grand masterpiece of homoerotic poetry';[7] on the other hand there are still many readers
who would totally oppose this suggestion. In 1989 A. L. Rowse
wrote, with that sublime self-assurance of which he was a master,

> Two of my dearest friends at Oxford, even at All Souls – have
> always wanted to think the Sonnets at least homo-erotic, and
> would not take telling from me. This failure on their part came
> from their not being acclimatized to Elizabethan language and
> usage: they were thinking of it in modern terms. With their
> Public School background they *wanted* to think the Sonnets
> homo-erotic; myself, open-minded, I would not mind if they
> were – but William Shakespeare makes it perfectly clear that
> they are not.[8]

If the 1890s represent a turning point, I am not aware of any
attempt to identify homosexuality in the texts of the plays, or to

portray it in performances of them, until the twentieth century; but documentation is comparatively slight until the early nineteenth century. And it would be surprising to find frank discussion of this topic in the Victorian period. It is inextricably bound up with the history of attitudes to sexuality. As Simon Shepherd remarks in a rather contortedly ironical essay, 'Neither the academic debate about [Shakespeare's] sexuality nor theatrical interpretations of homosexual scenes take place in a historical void.'[9]

I can claim no expertise in the history of attitudes to sexuality, but none is required to see that during the twentieth century an increasing amount of criticism devoted to explorations of the psychological subtexts of Shakespeare's plays was accompanied by a parallel increase in the number of portrayals of homosexuality in productions. I want to try to identify a few of the more prominent landmarks, and to consider some of their implications.

There are certain characters in Shakespeare whom it is particularly easy to identify with homosexuality. One is Richard II, whom Shakespeare portrays as being influenced for the bad by 'caterpillars of the commonwealth' (*Richard II*, 2.3.16), who are said, in an otherwise unexplained phrase, to have 'Made a divorce betwixt his queen and him, / Broke the possession of a royal bed' (3.1.12–13). It may be for this very reason that *Richard II* was little performed during the nineteenth century. Certainly critics frequently expressed moral disapproval of Richard: he offended against concepts of manliness. The play's growth in popularity dates from the performances given over nearly thirty years, starting in 1896, by Frank Benson, who was said by reviewers to have stressed what was described as the 'effeminate' side of Richard's nature.[10] This does not necessarily imply homosexuality, but it sounds like a euphemistic attempt to avoid mentioning the subject at a time when anything more explicit might have been unacceptable in polite circles. At least it suggests an ambivalence, or openness to interpretation, which is in keeping with the uncertainties within the text.

Later actors have been less guarded. According to Laurence Olivier – speaking informally – Michael Redgrave played Richard as 'an out-and-out pussy queer, with mincing gestures to match' (Fig. 10).[11]

This allusion to 'mincing gestures' alerts us to the fact that just as the presence of homosexuality in a text may be a matter of interpretation, so its presence in a performance is a matter not only of the way an actor behaves on stage but also of the way a spectator 'reads' his performance. Actual caressing, embracing, or kissing, may leave little room for doubt; there are many other kinds of signal which may be more or less explicit and in any case have to be interpreted, or decoded. We also have to allow for the fact that, in these days when the private lives of actors are rarely a closely guarded secret, the audience may transfer on to the character what it knows about the actor. At least four of the major actors of Richard II in England over the past half century or so are generally known to be, or to have been homosexual (I have in mind Sir Michael Redgrave – who was ambivalent – Sir John Gielgud, Sir Ian McKellen and Sir Derek Jacobi). They might have needed to make a special effort if they wished to make it clear that they were trying in performance to dissociate themselves from this view of Richard. (Oddly enough I can't think of any major actor before the twentieth century who was known to be homosexual – but the label had not yet been created.)

In the text, the relationship, whatever its precise nature may be, between Richard and his favourites is entirely unromantically

10. *Richard II*: Michael Redgrave as the King, Shakespeare Memorial
Theatre, 1951

portrayed. It is clearly associated with the less admirable aspects of Richard's character. In the later part of the play, when sympathy swings back to him, we see him in a tenderly loving relationship with his wife.

Other male characters in Shakespeare openly betray idealized intensity of affection for other men comparable to that expressed by the persona of the sonnets, and with a similar effect on their interpreters. One is Antonio, a comparatively minor character in *Twelfth Night*, whom I quoted earlier. It is easy to portray him as an older man enamoured of a younger Sebastian who only partly understands the nature of Antonio's affection, and such a portrayal would be very much in keeping with the tone of a play that is full of the pain of unrequited love. Indeed, Stephen Orgel has described Antonio and Sebastian as

> the only overtly homosexual couple in Shakespeare except for Achilles and Patroclus. What the presence of Antonio and Sebastian acknowledges, in a play that has at its center a man wooing a man, is that men *do* fall in love with other men. 'You are betrothed,' Sebastian tells Olivia, 'both to a maid and man,' recalling the master-mistress of Shakespeare's passion in the Sonnets.[12]

The relationship exists in Antonio's silences no less than in his words. Writing of Peter Gill's Stratford production in 1974, Lois Potter remarks

> It has become customary in modern productions to emphasise the isolation of Antonio, like his counterpart in *The Merchant of Venice*, from final happiness. In Barton's production, he went off in a different direction from the two couples at the end. In the context of a frankly erotic world like that of Gill's

production, his reactions were a particularly important part of the final scene. During Viola's brief account of herself to Sebastian . . . Antonio turned to look out front. The implication, I think, was that he had just tasted the fruit of the Tree of Knowledge; he realised, that is, the nature and hopelessness of his feelings for Sebastian. The play ended with a dance into which the lovers drew him for a while; then they went out behind the Narcissus panel [the stage set featured a large, symbolical painting of Narcissus] . . . it closed behind them, and Antonio was left staring at it as Feste sang the closing song. This was the most insistent treatment of the homosexual possibilities latent in the renaissance ideal of friendship. Like Irving's Malvolio, it brings out something which is potentially rather than actually present in the text.[13]

Since then however, in Lindsay Posner's Stratford production of 2001, that 'something' was brought out far more clearly not at the end of the play but in Antonio's first appearance. He and Sebastian appeared on a bed in which they had clearly just slept together, and it would have been a very unsophisticated spectator who did not assume both from this and from the desire visible in Antonio's farewells to his partner that they had enjoyed a night of love (Fig. 11).[14]

More prominent is that other Antonio, the merchant of Venice, an unattached man who takes no part in the wooing games of the play and who is unassimilated into its happy ending. At its opening he is portrayed as inexplicably melancholy; he says 'Fie, fie' (1.1.46) – whatever that may imply – when it is suggested that his sadness may be caused by love; soon we learn that his close friend Bassanio, for whom he clearly feels more than commonplace affection, is seeking his financial help – which Antonio unhesitatingly offers 'to the uttermost' (1.1.181) – in pursuing

77

11. 'Will you stay no longer, nor will you not that I go with you?'
Twelfth Night, 2.1.1–2: Antonio (Joseph Mydell) and Sebastian
(Ben Meyjes); Royal Shakespeare Theatre, 2001

his courtship of Portia. Later, Solanio speaks wonderingly of Antonio's love for Bassanio:

SALARIO
. . .
I saw Bassanio and Antonio part.
Bassanio told him he would make some speed
Of his return. He answered, 'Do not so.
Slubber not business for my sake, Bassanio,
But stay the very riping of the time;
And for the Jew's bond which he hath of me,
Let it not enter in your mind of love.
Be merry, and employ your chiefest thoughts
To courtship and such fair ostents of love
As shall conveniently become you there.'
And even there, his eye being big with tears,
Turning his face, he put his hand behind him
And, with affection wondrous sensible,
He wrung Bassanio's hand; and so they parted.

SOLANIO
I think he only loves the world for him.

(*The Merchant of Venice*, 2.8.36–50 (Fig. 12))

In the trial scene Antonio betrays an instinct for self-sacrifice that may well seem more than normal, describing himself as a 'tainted wether of the flock' and baring his breast to Shylock's knife. Expecting death, he seems to be casting himself as Portia's competitor in love:

Commend me to your honourable wife.
Tell her the process of Antonio's end.
Say how I loved you. Speak me fair in death,
And when the tale is told, bid her be judge
Whether Bassanio had not once a love.
Repent but you that you shall lose your friend,
And he repents not that he pays your debt;

12. *The Merchant of Venice*: Antonio (Julian Curry) and Bassanio
(Scott Handy), Royal Shakespeare Theatre, 1997

> For if the Jew do cut but deep enough,
> I'll pay it instantly, with all my heart. (4.1.270–8)

Paul Hammond, in his excellent study *Figuring Sex Between Men from Shakespeare to Rochester*, offers a subtle discussion of meanings that may lie behind this passage.

> What exactly 'friend' means here, and whether 'love' means
> 'experience of love' or 'sexual partner' is impossible to
> determine. One editor glosses 'love' as 'friend', with a
> cross-reference to Sonnet 13, thus neatly saving both texts
> from any suspicion of impropriety. Lorenzo had described
> Antonio to Portia as 'How true a gentleman . . . / How dere a
> lover of my Lord your Husband', to which Portia replies that
> she knows Antonio 'to be the bosome lover of my Lord'. All
> the characters recognize Antonio's special love for Bassanio,

but what exactly it amounts to, no one says. Once again, the public language of male friendship contains within it the possibility of a more private and sexual relation. (pp. 93–4)

It is understandable, then, that the relationship between Antonio and Bassanio is one of those most frequently treated in performance as homoerotic. Some productions suggest that the sexual element is present only in Antonio; others that the relationship is mutual; some even that Bassanio is cynically exploiting Antonio's love for him. As I have suggested, it is not always easy to be sure whether the impression one receives from a performance is intended by the play's interpreters or whether one is reading it in oneself. Bill Alexander's 1987 Stratford production, which had Antony Sher as Shylock, made it clear that Antonio's melancholy stemmed from frustrated sexual desire for Bassanio. Antonio reeled as Bassanio spoke of his admiration for Portia and kissed him with despairing passion but little response as they parted. As I read it, Antonio was to be understood as a depressive homosexual and the manner in which Bassanio reciprocated his affection – which is undeniable in the lines – did not preclude the thought that they might have had a consummated physical relationship which was coming to an end because Bassanio had fallen in love with Portia.

This reading between the lines was by no means new to this production and is indeed entirely understandable. Even in a production such as Peter Hall's at the Phoenix Theatre, London, in 1989, in which Dustin Hoffman played Shylock, and which determinedly refrained from hinting at a physical relationship between Antonio and Bassanio, a modern audience is likely to draw its own inferences; and it is arguable that such a production serves Shakespeare better by leaving more to the imagination.

The matter is sensitively discussed in an article on the play by Keith Geary, who writes that although the opening scene between Antonio and Bassanio

> is tense with an unspoken loosening of ties, it is not a love-scene . . . it is now common for Antonio and Bassanio to kiss in this scene and others. Such directorial touches both recognize an important element in the play and falsify the manner in which Shakespeare presents it. There is no justification in the text for such intimate physical contact – behaviour which on the Elizabethan stage would direct the audience's anti-homosexual feelings against the characters involved, a response on which the design of Marlowe's *Edward II* is founded. What the text does make clear is that the relationship between Antonio and Bassanio is of great intensity, of love, most importantly on Antonio's side, and strong enough for his claims to counterbalance those of Bassanio's newly established relationship with Portia . . .[15]

Whatever happened on Shakespeare's stage, it is arguable that physical demonstrativeness may be justifiable in a modern production. But I found it surprising in Bill Alexander's that those two deeply unmemorable characters Salerio and Solanio were also portrayed as homosexual, kissing each other in the only scene they have alone together. This was a production in which the Christians were somewhat unsympathetically presented, no doubt as a way of preserving a moral balance within the play, and it seemed to me surprising and regrettable at this point in our cultural history that homosexuality should be presented as if it would automatically be regarded as a symbol of corruption or decadence within the society.

If Bassanio starts off as Antonio's lover, there is no question that he ends as Portia's husband. There are a number of plays in which an internal journey from homosexuality to heterosexuality – or at least, to put it less explicitly, a transition from male bonding to the establishment of a heterosexual relationship – may be read between the lines. This was done with Orsino in the Peter Gill production of *Twelfth Night* to which I have referred. In this play it is particularly easy to make plausible because of the ambivalences inherent in Orsino's attraction to Viola in her disguise as a boy. It has been tried out too with the insecure lovers of *The Two Gentlemen of Verona*. And something like it may be seen in the complex relationship between Paroles and Bertram in *All's Well that Ends Well*.

Many actors experience a need to create a fictional scenario of the life between and behind the scenes of the character they impersonate, and this is particularly understandable in the case of characters who may seem underwritten, lacking motivation for their actions. Don John, in *Much Ado About Nothing*, is one of these. He is villainous, an outsider. He appears to resent the 'most exquisite' Claudio's impending marriage to Hero, speaks dismissively of her as 'A very forward March chick' (1.3.46, 52), and plots successfully to deceive Claudio into repudiating her at the altar. The text offers no clear explanation; more than one actor has contrived to suggest that he is motivated by repressed desire for Claudio. Of Ian McDiarmid's interpretation of Don John at Stratford in 1976, Pamela Mason writes: 'He was fastidious and somewhat effeminate, flicking the dust from a chair with a handkerchief before sitting down. There was also a suggestion of sexual repression as a motive for his actions.'[16]

The same play includes in Don Pedro a character who has something in common with the Antonio of *The Merchant of Venice*; though he is not so conspicuously melancholy, he too helps to forward other men's courtship but himself ends the play unmarried. But, as Simon Shepherd remarks of Don Pedro and of both the Antonios, 'In no case does [Shakespeare's] text give them lines that call attention to themselves as casualties.'[17]

A tiny snatch of dialogue in which Don Pedro is involved may serve as an illustration of the way in which text may be explored for subtextual pointers to a character's state of mind. Hero has accepted Claudio's offer of marriage. Beatrice laments that she is growing into an old maid. Don Pedro offers to 'get' her a husband, and she replies punningly, 'I would rather have one of your father's getting.' Her next words are 'hath your grace ne'er a brother like you?' This is obviously a compliment to Don Pedro, though a little pause before Beatrice utters it might be made to convey embarrassment lest she appears to have been dropping a serious hint. Pedro responds with 'Will you have me, lady?' Is this no more than a conventional gallantry, or is he taking an opportunity to convey something deeper? She replies 'No, my lord, unless I might have another for working days' (2.1.302–7). Is she simply sustaining an emptily flirtatious exchange? Is she covering the fact that she meant what she said more seriously than her tone of voice might have implied? Or is she even, perhaps, apologizing for having addressed a man who, she knew, would never marry, in the tone of heterosexual badinage? These are among the options that performers of the role might explore. In Gregory Doran's production at Stratford in 2002, Clive Wood expertly portrayed a gently and sympathetically camp Don Pedro whose close relationship with Claudio hinted at far more than it stated.

The character who – at least since Coleridge spoke of his 'motiveless malignity' – has most notoriously called for psychological investigation is Iago, in *Othello*. As it happens, he speaks what are surely the most homoerotically charged lines in

Shakespeare when, attempting to substantiate his imputation of Cassio's adultery with Desdemona, he tells Othello what happened when (as was not uncommon in Shakespeare's time) he shared Cassio's bed:

> I lay with Cassio lately,
> And being troubled with a raging tooth,
> I could not sleep. There are a kind of men
> So loose of soul that in their sleeps
> Will mutter their affairs. One of this kind is Cassio.
> In sleep I heard him say 'Sweet Desdemona,
> Let us be wary, let us hide our loves',
> And then, sir, would he grip and wring my hand,
> Cry 'O, sweet creature!', then kiss me hard,
> As if he plucked up kisses by the roots,
> That grew upon my lips, lay his leg o'er my thigh,
> And sigh, and kiss, and then cry 'Cursèd fate,
> That gave thee to the Moor!' (3.3.418–30)

That straightforward description of one man making love to another – omitted in nineteenth- and early twentieth-century acting texts – is anaesthetized by its presentation as a heterosexual dream fantasy. Presumably we are to take it that Iago remained the detached observer throughout this potentially disturbing, if not arousing, experience – unless, that is, the whole episode is of his own invention, in which case it might represent the fantasy of a diseased mind. Could an actor convey this? Perhaps so. If it is what Shakespeare meant, should he not have written something into the text to clarify it? But does it matter what Shakespeare meant if this is an interpretation to which the text is susceptible? These are questions that I shall not try to answer.

Besides Cassio, there are at least two other characters in the play to whom Iago might be represented as being sexually attracted – Roderigo, who has a dependent relationship with him, and Othello himself. It is recorded that when Laurence Olivier was to play Iago under the direction of Tyrone Guthrie in 1938 they went together to interview Ernest Jones, who had written a distinguished Freudian interpretation of *Hamlet*, and who told them that 'to his mind the clue to the play was not Iago's hatred for Othello, but his deep affection for him. His jealousy was not because he envied Othello's position, not because he was in love with Desdemona, but because he himself possessed a subconscious affection for the Moor, the homosexual foundation of which he did not understand.'[18] Olivier attempted to translate this interpretation into theatrical terms, with but limited success. In an interview with Kenneth Tynan he described a rehearsal with his Othello, Ralph Richardson, in which, 'losing all control of myself, I flung my arms round Ralph's neck and kissed him. Whereat Ralph, more in sorrow than in anger, sort of patted me and said, "Dear fellow, dear boy", much more pitying me for having lost control of myself, than despising me for being a very bad actor.'[19]

Later actors too have tried to suggest homosexual impulses within Iago's contorted psychosexual makeup. Playing the role to Olivier's Othello in 1964, Frank Finlay, according to Tynan, deduced that Iago had been 'impotent for years – hence his loathing of Othello's sexuality and his alienation from Emilia'.

> This Iago cannot tolerate Emilia's hands on him, although he often takes Roderigo's hand in his . . . obsessed with sexual longings that he apparently cannot fulfill [sic], he is strangely drawn to those whom he envies and hates. Towards the strong black man whose virility he cannot imitate, his ambivalence is unforgettably clarified when, after Othello breaks down and 'falls' to the ground in a trance, Iago straddles him and thrusts

the handle of a dagger into his victim's mouth. Shortly afterwards, when the arrival of Lodovico is announced, Iago wipes the spittle from Othello's tongue.[20]

Iago is one of several major characters in Shakespeare of whom it can reasonably be claimed that the complexity of their portrayal invites subtextual exploration of their psychological makeup. Another is Leontes in *The Winter's Tale*. In the opening scene of the play he is, apparently, suddenly afflicted with an obsessive belief that his wife, Hermione, is committing adultery with his oldest and closest friend, Polixenes. (I say apparently because there have been attempts to prove that he is jealous from the start, as John Gielgud played him in Peter Brook's 1951 London production.) Whereas Othello's jealousy is deliberately provoked by Iago (even though some critics would argue that it is already latent in Othello's mind), Leontes' seems to come upon him from within. It was, I believe, J. I. M. Stewart – (also known, in his capacity as a writer of detective stories, as Michael Innes) – who, in a book first published in 1949, citing Freud on jealousy, first proposed that Leontes' behaviour may be interpreted as following 'a typical paranoid pattern'. He explained that

> An early fixation of his affections upon his friend, long dormant, is reawakened in Leontes – though without being brought to conscious focus – by that friend's actual presence for the first time since their 'twyn'd' boyhood. An unconscious conflict ensues and the issue is behaviour having as its object the violent repudiation of the newly reactivated homosexual component in his own character. In other words, Leontes projects upon his wife the desires he has to repudiate in himself.[21]

A more recent critic calls this 'the standard psychoanalytic explanation for Leontes' madness, that Leontes imagines Hermione fulfilling his own desire to have sexual intercourse with Polixenes'.[22] Although, however, many actors have, inevitably, portrayed Leontes as a highly neurotic character, I am not aware of any who have attempted to convey this interpretation in performance. It is only in the play's opening and closing scenes that the two men are on stage together, so there is not much opportunity to explore the relationship between them.

I suggested that the only unquestionable allusion to a homosexual relationship in Shakespeare occurs in *Troilus and Cressida*. The friendship between Achilles and Patroclus was legendary; its precise nature was much discussed. One interpretation of it is put into the mouth of the scurrilous, railing Thersites. As Partridge noted (pp. 68–9 above), he says to Patroclus 'Thou art thought to be Achilles' male varlet', 'his masculine whore'. Patroclus neither accepts nor denies the charge. Characteristically of this play, Thersites' terminology is reductionist. Achilles and Patroclus might be lovers without Patroclus being regarded as a whore; or they might just be good friends. It may be thought characteristic of Shakespeare that he leaves the question open. It may be thought equally characteristic of later twentieth-century attitudes to plump firmly for Thersites' view. Thus, for example, A. P. Rossiter, in a book published in 1961, wrote that Achilles fights 'only because his catamite Patroclus is killed'[23] – one notes the loaded word 'catamite' – and Jan Kott, in 1964, wrote homophobically of the relationship in terms that might be descriptive of a German expressionist production: 'The great Achilles, the heroic Achilles, the legendary Achilles wallows in his bed with his male tart – Patroclus. He is a homosexual, he is boastful, stupid, and quarrelsome like an old hag.'[24] Maybe so, but the idea that they are in bed together is not in the stage directions or even, explicitly, in the lines. In 1968 the theatre critic W. A. Darlington, reacting to a John Barton production, wrote that 'Shakespeare nowhere shows any sign of intending to make homosexuals of the two characters. This idea has been read into the play by modern theatrical directors'[25] – but it could be retorted that Thersites had got there before them. And it might be fairer to say that along with Thersites' reductive allusion to the relationship between the two men, Shakespeare places a more charitable, even romantic view of it in the mouth of Patroclus himself: after Ulysses has taunted Achilles with cowardice, Patroclus remarks:

> To this effect, Achilles, have I moved you.
> A woman impudent and mannish grown
> Is not more loathed than an effeminate man
> In time of action. I stand condemned for this.
> They think my little stomach to the war
> And your great love to me restrains you thus.
> Sweet, rouse yourself, and the weak wanton Cupid
> Shall from your neck unloose his amorous fold
> And like a dew-drop from the lion's mane
> Be shook to air. (3.3.209–18)

Patroclus is pleading with Achilles not to let his love for Polyxena divert him from his martial exploits – 'effeminate' meant 'over-influenced by women' – so although it is easy to read or hear the reference to Cupid's 'amorous fold' in relation to Patroclus, it more likely refers to Polyxena. But the allusion to Achilles' 'great love' for Patroclus is clear. I find it difficult to believe that in writing these lines Shakespeare was not imagining a true love relationship between the men in the fullest sense of the word.

One of the remarkable things about *Troilus and Cressida* is that it has no stage history before the twentieth century, so we can't refer to a theatrical tradition. The author of an unpublished stage history of the play remarks that it was in a Marlowe Society production, by George Rylands, in 1940 that 'Patroclus for the first time in the play's stage history drew the attention of the critics by a wild display of bisexual allure, more pathic than pathetic.'[26] According to Ralph Berry, Tyrone Guthrie – an interesting figure in the psychological interpretation of Shakespeare's text in performance – in his 1956 production presented Patroclus 'as homosexual only'.[27] The classic Peter Hall/John Barton production of 1960 had Patrick Allen as a robustly handsome Achilles and Dinsdale Landen as a willowy, blond Patroclus. Simon Shepherd, remarking that the 'grape-eating Achilles' may have been taken from a Greek vase, suggests that 'Patroclus with his glistening blond hair comes from a homo physique mag (the homo ghetto regularly used "high art" to make legitimate its illicit sex objects)'; he admits nevertheless that it might 'have been possible to miss the stereotype'[28] behind the Patroclus, and memory tells me that, although the appearance of the two men may have been calculated to suggest a relationship familiar enough to contemporary audiences, there was nothing explicitly sexual about it. This does not reduce its potential eroticism (Fig. 13). To quote Shepherd again, 'The male body can be safely erotic for as long as homosexuality is damned' (p. 109). By the time that John Barton directed the play in 1968, the Sexual Revolution had taken place and, we read, 'No element of the production was as widely discussed as Alan Howard's portrayal of Achilles. Shaved of all body hair, dressed in assorted "camp" outfits, Achilles was the quintessential symbol of Greek decadence . . . Achilles and Patroclus acted out a travesty of the Menelaus-Helen wedding for which the war was fought; the prompt copy describes the moment . . . "Myrmidons pull away and form wedding arch as Patroclus and Achilles rise . . . and exit camping." '[29] And that doesn't mean they were wearing rucksacks.

13. *Troilus and Cressida*, 3.3: Achilles (Patrick Allen) and Patroclus (Dinsdale Landen), with Ulysses (Eric Porter) in the production directed by John Barton and Peter Hall, Shakespeare Memorial Theatre, 1960

It is instructive in considering the difference between directorial intention and audience reaction that John Barton felt misunderstood; he is quoted as saying:

> We were attacked for presenting Achilles as an effeminate homosexual, which was something that had never entered our minds. We saw him as bisexual, a view that is surely embodied in Shakespeare's play and is also the view which the Elizabethan audience would have taken. What we did was to show him playing at effeminacy and homosexuality in order to mock and outrage the Greek generals.[30]

It must, I suggest, be regarded as a failure of execution if audiences were not given enough clues to enable them to discern that Achilles was meant to be acting a part.

It was said that the battle scenes in John Barton's production of *Troilus* 'became homosexual dances that joined the forces of Venus and Mars'.[31] This relates to one of the quotations with which I opened my discussion, the passage in *Coriolanus* in which Aufidius, greeting his former enemy, says:

> Here I clip
> The anvil of my sword, and do contest
> As hotly and as nobly with thy love
> As ever in ambitious strength I did
> Contend against thy valour. Know thou first,
> I loved the maid I married; never man
> Sighed truer breath. But that I see thee here,
> Thou noble thing, more dances my rapt heart
> Than when I first my wedded mistress saw
> Bestride my threshold. (4.5.110–19)

The homoerotic implications are, I take it, unmistakable, even though with Shakespeare's characteristic – I might even say irritating – even-handedness, they are accompanied by an assertion of heterosexuality, and it is understandable that they have been brought to the surface in productions. They were certainly there in Tyrone Guthrie's under-documented 1963 production at Nottingham, which I saw, and Roger Warren's description of the fight between the two men in Elijah Moshinsky's television production interestingly illustrates how subtext can be brought to the surface:

> Coriolanus and Aufidius fought the duel virtually naked. After they had beaten the weapons out of each other's hands, they continued to grapple, their hands around one another's throats – but the stranglehold became almost an embrace: as they stared infatuated into each other's eyes, there was a cross-cut back to Rome. The effect was repeated when Coriolanus went to Antium. Aufidius took Coriolanus by the throat before embracing him and massaging his chest slowly and intently as he said that to see Coriolanus there 'more dances my rapt heart / Than when I first my wedded mistress saw / Bestride my threshold'.[32]

Another reviewer felt that it was over-explicit: 'Playing it with so many overtly homosexual caresses removes some of the ambiguity that hovers over the heroic ideal in Shakespeare's text. It literalizes and excessively motivates what is merely an undertone in the text.'[33] But if the subject were to be at all fully treated, it would have to be allowed that any psychological interpretation of the play would relate the lines I have cited to features of Coriolanus' character, such as the emotional immaturity that is suggested by his mother's domination over him and by the taunts of 'boy' directed against him. Coriolanus is one of Shakespeare's characters most susceptible to psychological

14. 'Here I clip / The anvil of my sword, and do contest / As hotly and as nobly with thy love / As ever in ambitious strength I did / Contend against thy valour': *Coriolanus*, 4.5.110–14. Coriolanus (Ian Hogg) and Aufidius (Patrick Stewart), Royal Shakespeare Theatre, 1972, directed by Trevor Nunn

theorizing, just as he is also a character about whom the other characters of the play itself are constantly expressing opinions. If actors and directors are to be allowed the right of interpretation, the right to realize a subtext, then this is one that seems hard to deny (Fig. 14).

I have by no means exhausted my subject. Indeed I feel that I have done little more than scratch its surface. I have not mentioned the relationships of Hal and Falstaff, or of Hamlet and Horatio; Toby Robertson's 1973 production for Prospect Players of *Pericles* set in a male brothel, or Cheek by Jowl's 1986 *Twelfth Night*, or the public lavatory in Nick Hytner's 1987 Royal

Shakespeare Company production of *Measure for Measure*. And I have alluded to only a few of the many critical studies that are relevant to my subject. But I should like to end with a few general considerations.

There is, I take it, always a sexual element in the relationship between actors and actresses and their audiences. It may lie deep within their subconscious, but it will be there. It is a factor that can be exploited. I have seen actors (and actresses) flirt with their audiences. And indeed it may be said that Shakespeare himself encourages this in, especially, the Epilogue to *As You Like It*, when Rosalind – originally played by a boy – addresses the men in the audience:

> And I charge you, O men, for the love you bear to women – as I perceive by your simpering none of you hates them – that between you and the women the play may please. If I were a woman I would kiss as many of you as had beards that pleased me, complexions that liked me, and breaths that I defied not. And I am sure, as many as have good beards, or good faces, or sweet breaths will for my kind offer, when I make curtsy, bid me farewell.

I have seen performers use their roles as vehicles for a covert form of sexual exhibitionism. If we feel that this is done to the detriment of the play we have a right to object. On the other hand actors are, usually, portraying real people, people in whose lives sexuality must play a part, and it is entirely right that they should project these characters in their fullness. In doing so they will properly draw upon a play's subtext, and if they find homosexuality there they are right to project it so that their audiences recognize it. They may do so as part of the makeup of a generally sympathetic character – as is likely with the Antonios, or (unless they accept Thersites' point of view) Achilles and Patroclus; or

95

as part of a generally unsympathetic one, as is likely with Don John or Iago. Whether in doing so they can be said to be embodying Shakespeare's meaning is debatable. The meanings that we find in plays are culturally determined; some critics would say, entirely so. Still, some aspects of relationships are defined by the texts; others have to be sought under their surface. In exploring these texts, both actors and critics may draw on the findings of psychoanalysis, but dramatic characters are little more than extrapolations from the words of their creator (and even that word employs a metaphor that might be questioned). We cannot psychoanalyse a dramatic character; but we can fictionalize it, extend the process by which the playwright portrayed it, imagine a life beyond but consistent with the information supplied by the text.

In doing this we may be employing the text for a form of therapy – a working out of our own fantasies, a projection of our secret desires. It is a process that can be indulged in either by the audience or by the performers. For individual members of the audience – as indeed for readers – it is an entirely private process, impinging on none but themselves; for the performers it is a public act that will provoke responses and judgements that will be complexly related to the psychological makeup of those who witness them. To make explicit that which is, at the most, implicit in the text will close options for some but may excitingly objectify the perceptions of others. As human beings develop their ideas about human sexuality, so Shakespeare's plays go on yielding new depths of meaning, demonstrating relationships which hold the mirror up to more and more aspects of humanity.

Notes

INTRODUCTION

1. Such difficulties are entertainingly and illuminatingly illustrated by Kamila Shamsie's short story 'Shakespeare in my Garden: Reading *Measure for Measure* in a Pakistani Context', *Shakespeare Jahrbuch 2002* (Bochum: Verlag und Druckkonton Kamp, 2002), pp. 135–42.

2. The event is discussed in *Shakespeare Comes to Broadmoor: 'the Actors Are Come Hither': The Performance of Tragedy in a Secure Psychiatric Hospital*, ed. Murray Cox (London: Jessica Kingsley Publishers, 1992).

3. *Timon of Athens*, ed. John Jowett, The Oxford Shakespeare (Oxford: Oxford University Press, 2004), pp. 113–15.

4. Jan Kott, *Shakespeare Our Contemporary*, tr. Boleslaw Taborski, Preface by Peter Brook (London: Methuen & Co., 1964).

1 LEWD INTERPRETERS

1. Eric Partridge, *Shakespeare's Bawdy: A Literary and Psychological Essay and a Comprehensive Glossary* (London: Routledge & Kegan Paul, 1968), pp. 30–1.

2. E. A. M. Colman, *The Dramatic Use of Bawdy in Shakespeare* (London: Longman, 1974), p. 13 cites Thomas Dekker (with Thomas Middleton) *The Honest Whore*, Part One (1.2.4), *The Dramatic Works of Thomas Dekker*, ed. Fredson Bowers (Cambridge: Cambridge University Press, 1955).

3. Modernized from the reprint in Christopher Spencer, ed., *Five Restoration Adaptations of Shakespeare* (Urbana, IL: University of Illinois Press, 1965), p. 189.

4. Gerard Langbaine, *An Account of the English Dramatic Poets* (London, 1691; reprinted by The Scolar Press: Menston, 1971), p. 177.

5. *Shakespeare Adaptations: The Tempest, The Mock-Tempest, and King Lear*, with an Introduction and Notes by Montague Summers (London: Jonathan Cape, 1922), p. 58.

6. E. K. Chambers, ed., *The Shakespere Allusion-Book: A Collection of Allusions to Shakespeare from 1591 to 1700*, originally compiled by C. M. Ingleby, L. Toulmin

Smith, and F. J. Furnivall, 2 vols. (London: Oxford University Press, 1932), vol. II, p. 209.

7. *A New Variorum Edition of Shakespeare*, ed. Horace Howard Furness (Philadelphia: J. B. Lippincott, 1874), p. 91.

8. Gordon Williams, *A Glossary of Shakespeare's Sexual Language* (London: Athlone Press, 1997), p. 7.

9. *OED*: 'Sir T. Hanmer, in his edition of Shaks. (1744) suggested that in the three Shaks. passages *good yeare(s)* had the sense of the French "Disease", and was a "corruption" of *goujeres*, a hypothetical derivative of "the French word *gouje*, which signifies a common Camp-Trull". So far as the sense is concerned, this explanation is curiously plausible, as it seems to be applicable without any violence to all the examples of the word (cf. *what the pox* etc.). But there is no evidence that the definite meaning of "pox" was really intended by any of the writers who used the word; and the spurious form goujere or goujeer, has, however, found its way into many editions of Shakespere, and was adopted as the standard form in Johnson's Dict. 1755, and hence in every later Dict. which contains the word.'

10. Williams, *Glossary*, p. 7.

11. *Johnson on Shakespeare*, ed. Arthur Sherbo, 2 vols. (New Haven and London: Yale University Press, 1968), p. 946.

12. Robert Bridges, *Collected Essays Papers & c of Robert Bridges*, 30 parts (Oxford: Oxford University Press, 1927–36), I, p. 28.

13. Gary Taylor, *Reinventing Shakespeare: A Cultural History from the Restoration to the Present* (New York: Weidenfeld & Nicolson; London: Hogarth, 1990), pp. 207–8.

14. *The Family Shakspeare*, ed. Thomas Bowdler, 10 vols. (London: Longmans, Green & Co., 1878), vol. I, p. vii.

15. Edwin W. Marrs, Jr, ed., *The Letters of Charles and Mary Lamb*, 3 vols. (Ithaca and London: Cornell University Press, 1975–8), vol. II, p. 256 (Charles Lamb to William Wordsworth, 29 January 1807).

16. Charles and Mary Lamb, *Tales from Shakespeare* (London; New York: J. M. Dent & Sons; E. P. Dutton & Co., 1959), p. 2.

17. Bowdler, *The Family Shakspeare*, p. viii.

18. Helen Vendler, *The Art of Shakespeare's Sonnets* (Cambridge, MA and London: The Bellknap Press of Harvard University Press, 1997), p. 63.

19. A photograph of Zdenek Stepanek's Municipal Theatre production of 1927 reproduced in *Hamlet Through the Ages*, by Raymond Mander and Joe Mitchenson (London: Rockliff, 1952), p. 103, shows a draped couch or bed and an enormous, phallic lit candle. Arthur Colby Sprague and J. C. Trewin, *Shakespeare's Plays Today: Some Customs and Conventions of the Stage* (London: Sidgwick & Jackson, 1970), date the appearance of the bed a few years later: 'Within memory, one scene in a play of Shakespeare's has been newly located, by means, chiefly, of a single property. When Hamlet after the Play Scene is summoned to his mother's

"closet", it would have been, in Shakespeare's meaning of the word, to a private room merely. There is nothing in the lines to indicate that it is a bedchamber, and indeed the only mention of a bed is of the King's bed, which is certainly elsewhere. In the staging of the scene a chair is conspicuous in early pictures . . . In the 1920's an austere couch or sofa is added to the chair . . . Meanwhile, critical interest in the sexual and even Freudian aspects of the play has been mounting. It is in keeping that what used to be known as the Closet Scene becomes "the Bedroom scene" in Dover Wilson's *What Happens in Hamlet* (1935). An actual bed, predictably, was introduced in Gielgud's brilliant *Hamlet* in New York the next year . . .'; p. 19.

20. Williams, *Glossary*, p. 10.
21. Partridge, *Shakespeare's Bawdy*, p. 25.
22. Colman, *Bawdy in Shakespeare*, p. 13.
23. Frankie Rubinstein, *A Dictionary of Shakespeare's Sexual Puns and their Significance* (London and Basingstoke: Macmillan Press, 1984), p. ix.
24. Colman, *Bawdy in Shakespeare*, p. 14.
25. *Shakespeare's Plutarch*, ed. T. J. B. Spencer (Harmondsworth: Penguin, 1964), p. 312.
26. Bruce Thomas Boehrer, 'Bestial Buggery in *A Midsummer Night's Dream*', in *The Production of English Renaissance Culture*, ed. David Lee Miller, Sharon O'Dair and Harold Weber (Ithaca and London: Cornell University Press, 1994), pp. 123–50. A revised version appears in Boehrer's *Shakespeare Among the Animals: Nature and Society in the Drama of Early Modern England* (London: Palgrave Press, 2002).
27. Boehrer, *Shakespeare Among the Animals*, p. 41.
28. Boehrer, 'Bestial Buggery', p. 132.
29. Boehrer, *Shakespeare Among the Animals*, p. 48.
30. Boehrer, *Shakespeare Among the Animals*, p. 46.
31. Jan Kott, *The Bottom Translation: Marlowe and Shakespeare and the Carnival Tradition*, tr. Daniela Miedzyrzecka and Lillian Vallee (Evanston, IL: Northwestern University Press, 1987), p. 52.
32. James L. Calderwood, *A Midsummer Night's Dream* (Brighton: Harvester Wheatsheaf, 1992), p. 63.
33. Boehrer, 'Bestial Buggery', p. 132. This phrase does not occur in the revised version.
34. Patricia Parker, *Shakespeare from the Margins: Language, Culture, Context* (Chicago and London: University of Chicago Press, 1996), p. 95.
35. Parker's error results from a misreading of Rubinstein, *Dictionary*, p. 196.
36. Parker, *Shakespeare from the Margins*, p. 95, citing Wolfgang Franke, 'The Logic of the Double Entendre in *A Midsummer Night's Dream*', *Philological Quarterly*, 58 (1979), pp. 282–97.

37. Joseph W. Elsworth, ed., *Choyce Drollery* (Boston, Lincs: Roberts, 1876), p. 52 quoting the following:

> And when to town the tinker doth come,
> Oh, how the wanton wenches run,
> Some bring him basons, and some bring him bowles,
> All maids desire him to stop their holes.

This is cited by Francke but not by Parker.

38. Eric Partridge, *A Dictionary of Slang and Unconventional English* (London: George Routledge & Sons, 1937), p. 620. The 1967 Supplement to revised vol. II offers '2. Among schoolboys, in certain localities, it is a polite synonym of *prick*, penis: C. 20', p. 1290.

39. Parker, *Shakespeare from the Margins*, p. 95.

40. Jan Kott, *Shakespeare our Contemporary*, tr. Boleslaw Taborski, Preface by Peter Brook (London: Methuen & Co., 1964), p. 183.

2 THE ORIGINALITY OF SHAKESPEARE'S SONNETS

1. Sidney Lee, *Elizabethan Sonnets*, 2 vols. (Westminster: Archibald Constable, 1904).

2. Lee, *Elizabethan Sonnets*, vol. I, p. xx.

3. Michael R. G. Spiller, *The Development of the Sonnet: An Introduction* (London and New York: Routledge, 1992), p. 93.

4. See the table in Spiller, *Development of the Sonnet*, pp. 198–9.

5. Jill Levenson, ed., *Romeo and Juliet* (Oxford: Oxford University Press, 2000), Introduction, pp. 52–7.

6. Like four of the other poems in *Rosalynde*, it came to Lodge by way of the French sonneteer Philippe Desportes (1545–1606). Charles Whitworth, 'The Literary Career of Thomas Lodge' (unpublished Ph.D. thesis, University of Birmingham, 1978), p. 273.

7. Paul Hammond, *Figuring Sex between Men from Shakespeare to Rochester* (Oxford: Oxford University Press, 2002), p. 74.

8. Quotations are modernized from Richard Barnfield, *The Complete Poems*, ed. George Klawitter (London and Toronto: Associated University Presses, 1990), note to l. 113. He notes another echo of *Edward II* at l. 115.

9. Virgil, *Eclogues*, tr. C. Day Lewis (Oxford: Oxford University Press, 1983), p. 7.

10. Barnfield, *Complete Poems*, Sonnet 8, p. 126.

11. Barnfield, *Complete Poems*, Sonnet 11, p. 127, ll. 9–14.

12. William Percy, *Coelia*, Sonnet 5, ll. 11–12 in Lee, *Elizabethan Sonnets*, vol. II, p. 143.

13. Barnabe Barnes, *Parthenophil and Parthenophe*, Sonnet 63, ll. 10–14 in Lee, *Elizabethan Sonnets*, vol. I, p. 207.

14. *The Poems of Sir Philip Sidney*, ed. William A. Ringler, Jr (Oxford: Clarendon Press, 1962), p. 165 – 'Foole! said my Muse to me, looke in thy heart, and write': *Astrophil and Stella*, Sonnet 1, l. 14.

15. Lee, *Elizabethan Sonnets*, vol. I, p. xxxiv.

16. Lee, *Elizabethan Sonnets*, vol. II, p. 28.

17. In his chapter on Shakespeare's sonnets, Spiller says:

> Both the man and the woman are praised in conventional Petrarchan or courtly terms in some sonnets; but others make it clear that the speaker feels himself betrayed by the shameful conduct of the man and the sexual promiscuity of the woman.
>
> There is a precedent for the last aspect in Catullus' disastrous devotion to Lesbia, and hints of it in Wyatt's poetry, but the existence of two deeply flawed and unworthy lovers is fundamentally anti-Petrarchan, and appears nowhere else in the Elizabethan sonnet. (*Development of the Sonnet*, pp. 152–3)

18. Andrew Gurr, 'Shakespeare's First Poem: Sonnet 145', *Essays in Criticism*, 21 (1971), pp. 221–6.

19. Gary Taylor, 'Some Manuscripts of Shakespeare's Sonnets', *The Bulletin of the John Rylands Library*, 68 (1985), pp. 210–46.

20. Spiller, *Development of the Sonnet*, p. 156.

21. Margreta de Grazia, 'The Scandal of Shakespeare's Sonnets', *Shakespeare Survey*, 14 (1994), pp. 35–50; reprinted in *Shakespeare and Sexuality*, ed. Catherine M. S. Alexander and Stanley Wells (Cambridge: Cambridge University Press, 2001), pp. 146–67.

22. Helen Vendler, *The Art of Shakespeare's Sonnets* (Cambridge, MA and London: The Bellknap Press of Harvard University Press, 1997), p. 639.

23. *A New Variorum Edition of Shakespeare: The Sonnets*, ed. Hyder Edward Rollins, 2 vols. (Philadelphia: J. B. Lippincott Company, 1944), vol. II, p. 232.

24. George Chalmers, *An Apology for the Believers in the Shakspeare-Papers, which were Exhibited in Norfolk Street* (London: Thomas Egerton, 1797), pp. 60–1; cited in Rollins, *The Sonnets*, vol. II, pp. 248–9, discussed in M. Keevak, *Sexual Shakespeare* (Detroit: Wayne State University Press, 2001), pp. 29–38.

25. George Chalmers, *Supplemental Apology* (London: Thomas Egerton, 1799), pp. 55, 63.

26. Samuel Taylor Coleridge, *The Collected Works of Samuel Taylor Coleridge* (1969–), Vol. 12: *Marginalia* (London: Routledge, 1980), pp. 42–3, cited by Gregory Woods, *A History of Gay Literature*: *The Male Tradition* (New Haven and London: Yale University Press, 1998), p. 104.

27. Oscar Wilde, *The Portrait of Mr W. H.: The greatly enlarged version prepared by the Author after the appearance of the Story in 1889, but not published*, edited with an Introduction by Vyvyan Holland (London: Methuen & Co., 1921), pp. 43–4.

28. Samuel Butler, *Shakespeare's Sonnets Reconsidered* (London: Jonathan Cape, 1927), p. 159.

29. Butler, *Shakespeare's Sonnets*, p. x.

30. Rictor Norton, *The Homosexual Literary Tradition: An Interpretation* (New York: Revisionist Press, 1974), p. 250; cited in Woods, *History of Gay Literature*, p. 106.

31. Spiller, *Development of the Sonnet*, p. 155.

32. Stephen Orgel, *Impersonations: The Performance of Gender in Shakespeare's England* (Cambridge: Cambridge University Press, 1996), p. 57.

33. *The Sonnets and 'A Lover's Complaint'*, ed. John Kerrigan (New Penguin edition: Harmondsworth, 1969), note to Sonnet 20.

34. Spiller, *Development of the Sonnet*, p. 124.

3 'I THINK HE LOVES THE WORLD ONLY FOR HIM': MEN LOVING MEN IN SHAKESPEARE'S PLAYS

1. Eric Partridge, *Shakespeare's Bawdy: A Literary and Psychological Essay and a Comprehensive Glossary* (London: Routledge & Kegan Paul, 1968), p. 14.

2. Frankie Rubinstein, *A Dictionary of Shakespeare's Sexual Puns and their Significance* (London and Basingstoke: Macmillan Press, 1984).

3. Williams does not cite this sense in his Shakespeare *Glossary*, but finds many sexual nuances for 'cat' in his *Dictionary of Sexual Language and Imagery in Shakespeare and Stuart Literature*, 3 vols. (London: Athlone Press, 1994).

4. Michel Foucault, *The Will to Knowledge: The History of Sexuality*, Volume 1, tr. Robert Hurley (Harmondsworth: Penguin Books, 1998), p. 43.

5. Philip Larkin, 'Annus Mirabilis', in *Collected Poems* edited with an introduction by Anthony Thwaite (London: Faber & Faber / The Marvell Press, 1988), p. 167.

6. Samuel Butler, *Shakespeare's Sonnets Reconsidered* (London: Jonathan Cape, 1927), p. 159.

7. Joseph Pequigney, *Such is My Love: A Study of Shakespeare's Sonnets* (Chicago and London: University of Chicago Press, 1985), p. 1.

8. A. L. Rowse, *Discovering Shakespeare: A Chapter in Literary History* (London: Weidenfeld & Nicolson, 1989), pp. 18–19.

9. Simon Shepherd, 'Shakespeare's Private Drawer: Shakespeare and Homosexuality', in *The Shakespeare Myth*, ed. Graham Holderness (Manchester: Manchester University Press, 1988), pp. 96–109, p. 97.

10. Richard L. O'Connell, 'A Stage History of *Richard II*, 1800–1920', 2 vols. (unpublished Ph.D. thesis, University of Birmingham, 1958), vol. II, p. 119.

11. Malcolm Page, *Richard II: Text and Performance* (Atlantic Highlands, NJ: Humanities Press International, 1987), p. 49.

12. Stephen Orgel, *Impersonations: The Performance of Gender in Shakespeare's England* (Cambridge: Cambridge University Press, 1996), p. 51.

13. Lois Potter, *Twelfth Night: Text and Performance* (Basingstoke and London: Macmillan, 1985), p. 59.

14. Arguing that the scene is 'for the space of Antonio's memory, and the audience's imagination, not for the stage', Paul Hammond declares it 'a faux pas in the RSC's 2001 production when Act 2 scene 1 opened with Sebastian getting out of their shared bed, and dressing' (*Figuring Sex between Men from Shakespeare to Rochester* (Oxford: Oxford University Press, 2002), p. 100, n. 150).

15. Keith Geary, 'The Nature of Portia's Victory: Turning to Men in *The Merchant of Venice*', *Shakespeare Survey*, 37, pp. 55–68, pp. 59–60.

16. Pamela Mason, *Much Ado About Nothing: Text and Performance* (London, Basingstoke: Macmillan, 1992), pp. 62–3.

17. Shepherd, 'Shakespeare's Private Drawer', p. 102.

18. Marvin Rosenberg, *The Masks of Othello: The Search for the Identity of Othello, Iago, and Desdemona by Three Centuries of Actors and Critics* (Berkeley and Los Angeles: University of California Press; London: Cambridge University Press, 1961), p. 158.

19. Julie Hankey, *Othello: William Shakespeare*, Plays in Performance Series (Bristol: Bristol Classical Press, 1987), p. 133, n. 457 cites Olivier's interview with Kenneth Tynan first published in *Tulane Drama Review*, 9, 3 (Winter 1966), reprinted in Toby Cale and Helen Krich Chinoy, eds., *Actors on Acting* (revised ed. London: Peter Owen, 1970; 1978 reprint), pp. 410–17, pp. 413–14.

20. Martin L. Wine, *Othello: Text and Performance* (Basingstoke and London: Macmillan, 1984), p. 61.

21. J. I. M. Stewart, *Character and Motive in Shakespeare: Some Recent Appraisals Examined* (London, New York and Toronto: Longmans, Green & Co., 1949), p. 35.

22. W. T. MacCary, *Friends and Lovers: The Phenomenology of Desire in Shakespearean Comedy* (New York and Guildford: Columbia University Press, 1985), p. 206.

23. A. P. Rossiter, *Angel With Horns and Other Shakespearean Lectures*, ed. Graham Storey (London: Longmans, Green & Co., 1961), p. 137.

24. Jan Kott, *Shakespeare Our Contemporary*, tr. Boleslaw Taborski, Preface by Peter Brook (London: Methuen & Co., 1964), p. 62.

25. W. A. Darlington, review in the *Daily Telegraph*, 9 August 1968, cited by Michael L. Greenwald, *Directions by Indirections: John Barton of the Royal Shakespeare Company* (London and Toronto: Associated University Presses, 1985), p. 74.

26. Michael E. Kimberley, '*Troilus and Cressida* on the English Stage' (unpublished M.A. thesis, University of Birmingham, Shakespeare Institute, June 1968), p. 97.

27. Ralph Berry, *Changing Styles in Shakespeare* (London: George Allen & Unwin, 1981), p. 54.

28. Shepherd, 'Shakespeare's Private Drawer', p. 108.
29. Greenwald, *Directions by Indirections*, p. 73.
30. Greenwald, *Directions by Indirections*, p. 74.
31. Greenwald, *Directions by Indirections*, p. 71 cites D. A. N. Jones, 'Mars n' Venus', *Listener*, 15 August 1968.
32. Roger Warren, 'Shakespeare in England', *Shakespeare Quarterly*, 35 (Autumn 1984), pp. 334–40, p. 336.
33. Maurice Charney, 'Alan Howard in Moshinsky's *Coriolanus*', *Shakespeare on Film Newsletter*, 9, 1 (December 1984), pp. 1 and 5.

Further reading

Bray, Alan, *Homosexuality in Renaissance England* (London: Gay Men's Press, 1982)

Brown, John Russell, 'Representing Sexuality in Shakespeare's Plays', *New Theatre Quarterly*, 13, 51; reprinted in *Shakespeare and Sexuality*, ed. Catherine M. S. Alexander and Stanley Wells (Cambridge: Cambridge University Press, 2001), pp. 146–67

Colman, E. A. M., *The Dramatic Use of Bawdy in Shakespeare* (London: Longman, 1974)

Dash, Irene, *Wooing, Wedding and Power: Women in Shakespeare's Plays* (New York: Columbia University Press, 1981)

de Grazia, Margreta, 'The Scandal of Shakespeare's Sonnets', *Shakespeare Survey*, 14 (1994), pp. 35–50; reprinted in *Shakespeare and Sexuality*, ed. Catherine M. S. Alexander and Stanley Wells (Cambridge: Cambridge University Press, 2001), pp. 146–67

DiGangi, Mario, *The Homoerotics of Early Modern Drama* (Cambridge: Cambridge University Press, 1997)

Hammond, Paul, *Figuring Sex between Men from Shakespeare to Rochester* (Oxford: Oxford University Press, 2002)

Hammond, Paul, *Love Between Men in English Literature* (Basingstoke: Macmillan, 1996)

Keevak, M., *Sexual Shakespeare* (Detroit: Wayne State University Press, 2001)

MacCary, W. T., *Friends and Lovers: The Phenomenology of Desire in Shakespearean Comedy* (New York and Guildford: Columbia University Press, 1985)

Mahood, Molly M., *Shakespeare's Wordplay* (London: Methuen, 1957)

Norton, Rictor, *The Homosexual Literary Tradition: An Interpretation* (New York: Revisionist Press, 1974)

Orgel, Stephen, *Impersonations: The Performance of Gender in Shakespeare's England* (Cambridge: Cambridge University Press, 1996)

Partridge, Eric, *Shakespeare's Bawdy: A Literary and Psychological Essay and a Comprehensive Glossary* (London: Routledge & Kegan Paul, 1968)

Pequigney, Joseph, *Such is My Love: A Study of Shakespeare's Sonnets* (Chicago and London: University of Chicago Press, 1985)

Shepherd, Simon, 'Shakespeare's Private Drawer: Shakespeare and Homosexuality', in *The Shakespeare Myth*, ed. Graham Holderness (Manchester: Manchester University Press, 1988), pp. 96–109

Smith, Bruce R., *Homosexual Desire in Shakespeare's England: A Cultural Poetics.* With a new Preface (Chicago: Chicago University Press, 1991, 1994)

Spiller, Michael R. G., *The Development of the Sonnet: An Introduction* (London and New York: Routledge, 1992)

Stewart, J. I. M., *Character and Motive in Shakespeare: Some Recent Appraisals Examined* (London, New York and Toronto: Longmans, Green & Co., 1949)

Traub, Valerie, *Desire and Anxiety: Circulations of Sexuality in Shakespearean Drama* (London: Routledge, 1992)

Wilde, Oscar, *The Portrait of Mr W. H.: The greatly enlarged version prepared by the Author after the appearance of the Story in 1889, but not published*, edited with an Introduction by Vyvyan Holland (London: Methuen & Co., 1921)

Williams, Gordon, *A Glossary of Shakespeare's Sexual Language* (London: Athlone Press, 1997)

Woods, Gregory, *A History of Gay Literature: The Male Tradition* (New Haven and London: Yale University Press, 1998)

Index